Expert Fly- Tying

*Paul N. Fling
& Donald L. Puterbaugh*

Sterling Publishing Co., Inc. New York

For Bob Damico whose friendship has enriched our lives on and off the stream.

Library of Congress Cataloging in Publication Data

Fling, Paul N.
  Expert fly-tying.

  Bibliography: p.
  Includes index.
  1. Fly tying. I. Puterbaugh, Donald L. II. Title.
SH451.F563   688.7′912   81-85025
ISBN 0-8069-7580-6 (pbk.)   AACR2

Copyright © 1982 by Sterling Publishing Co., Inc.
Two Park Avenue, New York, N.Y. 10016
Distributed in Australia by Oak Tree Press Co., Ltd.
P.O. Box K514 Haymarket, Sydney 2000, N.S.W.
Distributed in the United Kingdom by Blandford Press
Link House, West Street, Poole, Dorset BH15 1LL, England
Distributed in Canada by Oak Tree Press Ltd.
‰ Canadian Manda Group, 215 Lakeshore Boulevard East
Toronto, Ontario M5A 3W9
Manufactured in the United States of America

Contents

*Color plates face
pages* 48 & 49.

Foreword

Given the highly critical and judgmental nature of the fly-tying community, I would rather reveal the deficiencies and aberrations in my sex life than the faults and weaknesses in my fly-tying procedures. I would, for example, prefer to admit an affinity for black leather in the boudoir than a dependency upon the whip finisher at my fly-tying station. In fact—if I may push this analogy even closer to the bizarre edge of contemporary reality—sexual confessions in print are so commonplace as to arouse little more controversy than the ingredients on a box of cornflakes. But "woe betide" the fly tyer who discloses that he would rather carve balsa-wood bass plugs than attempt to engineer a size 18 Parachute Humpy.

There is no denying that the upper echelon in fly-tying society can be a hard and ornery lot. That's why it is such a pleasure to have been asked to write the Foreword to this book. The authors, Paul Fling and Don Puterbaugh, are not among that breed of cat—the imperious lordship of the high hackle art—who look down their noses at anyone who has not mastered throwing half-hitches with two fingers and one eye closed in the dark room immediately after engulfing two double-dry martinis. Fling and Puterbaugh do not make iconoclastic directives nor do they mistake preaching for teaching.

Rather than assume the specific needs of the reader, doling out information with pontifical authority, they have compiled a fly-tying how-to volume which simply and directly tells it A-L-L. Good educators worth their weight in bindery glue, Fling and Puterbaugh present a catalogue of alternatives. It is up to the individual reader to develop the attitudes, incorporate methods, and select pertinent detail regarding everything in the realm of fly-tying from the bewildering array of sadistic appearing hardware to the inevitable brain damage inherent in seeking professional status as a fly tyer.

They have made it possible for the fly tyer to cultivate and hone his skills by referring to a single, all-encompassing, source book rather than a helter-skelter gathering of magazines, books, periodicals, pamphlets, bulletins, lectures, and dogma expounded by self-aggrandizing experts. Fling and Puterbaugh are kind and gentle teachers (in the Socratic tradition) who use words and pictures as an honest mode for examining the strange and obsessive details of a highly technical hobby.

> "The time has come," the Walrus said,
>   "To talk of many things:
> Of shoes—and ships—and sealing wax—
>   Of cabbages—and kings—
> And why the sea is boiling hot—
>   And whether pigs have wings."
>   *Lewis Carroll*

Due to the extraordinary efforts of Paul Fling and Don Puterbaugh, as regards the fanatical universe of fly-tying, "The time has come . . ."

Don Roberts

Preface

Although we have really intended this book for the more advanced tyer, we also hope that we haven't lost the ability to convey the methods used to assemble a fly in a simple, easy-to-understand manner. Just where the dividing line falls between the beginner, the intermediate, and the advanced fly tyer is no clearer now than when we started the project. Our intent was to provide a single point of reference where you could find the knowledge to enable you to put together almost any pattern that you come across and give you the methods needed to develop your own innovative patterns to suit your particular fishing needs. We can only hope that we have covered enough different techniques and methods to present one that is "natural" for you.

Leaning heavily on the philosophy of our first book, *The Basic Manual of Fly-Tying,* we have not set out to present a bewildering number of patterns for the tyer. Our feeling is that fly-tying is like cooking, if you have the necessary ingredients (materials), and the basic culinary skills (techniques), then all that you require is a recipe to put together the fare—and a pattern is nothing more than a recipe. John Younger, in his book, *On River Angling for Salmon and Trout,* stated this philosophy quite well when he wrote: "Thus will be avoided all insignificant and endless enumeration and invention of names to flies, which rather tend to bewilder the reader's imagination, than prove instructive to the individual desirous of practical information." Those words were written in 1839 . . . well spoken, John!

In addition to tying techniques, we have attempted to provide the reader with the most complete information that we could assemble about the materials and tools used by the fly tyer. In each case, we went directly to the source for the information. Manufacturers of vises loaned us samples of their models and we used them enough to become accustomed to their individual features. We also asked each of the companies to tell us why they considered their product better than the others and then compared those "strengths" to the competition. Tools were handled in the same manner, as were the materials. Hooks presented a real dilemma; virtually none of the books on fly-tying agree on just exactly what the sizing standards are for hooks. I was pleased to find that the reason for this seeming disparity had a very logical root: There simply is no standard. We have attempted to work around that by contacting the major manufacturers and have given the standards used by each one.

All of this research required a lot of correspondence and, therefore, a lot of time, but we feel that it was well worth it if it saves you some time and trouble in deciding what and which of the myriad of offerings is best for your tying bench. And yes, some of the companies *did* allow us to keep the materials and tools that they provided us; but that was by their choice, and such offerings were never part of the "price" for getting their product mentioned in the book. In fact, some of the items that most impressed us were provided only on loan.

It would have been impossible for us to have sampled all of the tools and materials without the help of these companies and we thank them all. Perhaps the most rewarding part of the whole project was to find that the people who provide us with the items for our hobby are all honestly concerned with providing what is absolutely the best for you, the consumer. For the most part, they are just fly tyers and fishermen like ourselves, who have found what they consider is a better way of doing things and want to share it with everyone with like interests.

We would be remiss if we didn't also thank the many others who have provided a helping hand along the way. Bob Damico provided nearly all of the black and white photos and served, once again, as "devil's advocate" for the entire book. Don Roberts, of *Flyfishing the West* (he's everything an editor should be) allowed us to use the material on hackle that first appeared in that magazine. Ritch Philips provided the beautiful color photos, of which, the ones of hackle were also first seen in *Flyfishing the West*. Thanks, Pam for the hours at the typewriter. When things just weren't coming together as we'd like (a seemingly daily occurrence) our wives were the ones who suffered . . . they deserve canonization.

one
The Tyer's Tools

This chapter is meant simply to familiarize you with the available tools and provide enough information for you to better decide which of them you should consider as additions to your tying bench.

Basically, there are two kinds of tools—good ones and cheap junk! All of the good ones cost about the same, and the junk, surprisingly, sells for almost as much. If there is any area in the field of fly-tying where the buyer should beware, it is in the area of tools. Those that we have chosen for discussion are all of the highest quality, and we can heartily recommend them without fear that you will be dissatisfied. There may be some other manufacturers, producing tools of similar quality, and we'll try to explain enough about the aspects of quality for you to judge them for yourself.

Other than a vise, the only tools that the tyer really needs are scissors, hackle pliers, bobbin, and a bodkin (dubbing needle). On the other hand, the only "tools" that the fly fisherman really must have is a rod, reel, line, leader, and flies; but we all seem to find use for many more items than the basics. The same is true at the tying bench. Which of the tools are important enough for you to include on your bench depends a lot on the type of flies that you tie the most. If cut-wing dry flies are your pride and joy, you would certainly want to consider some wing formers. If, however, nymphs are your mainstay, you may opt for a dubbing twister instead of the wing former. In actuality, most of us end up with one of just about everything because who knows when you might want to tie a cut-wing dry? Just because you've been tying for ten years and haven't ever tied one is no rationale for not having the tool, is it?

The vise is the most important tool on the tying bench and, as such, deserves to be covered first in our discussion of the fly tyer's tools.

VISES

The first major purchase that the fly tyer usually considers after advancing beyond the beginning stage is a different vise. Those fancy, more expensive, models keep catching his eye in the stores, the magazine ads, and in the illustrated magazine articles. When he visits an International Sportsman's Exposition, the local Trout Unlimited Show, or the Federation of Fly Fishermen Conclave, it seems as if every fly tyer there is using a Price, HMH, Xuron, Renzetti, or some other make of expensive, "super-vise." This observation only enhances his conviction that in order to tie better flies, he simply must have a better vise than the one he is presently using.

Basically, this is a misconception. Any fly can be tied as perfectly on the Thompson Model A as on any other vise that can be bought at any price. In

9

fact, there are probably more flies tied (including those by commercial tyers) on the Thompson Model A per year than on all of the others combined.

Well, then, if the old Model A that you have been using will do the job as well as one of the "Porsches" of the fly-tying world, why should you consider laying out big bucks for one of them?

Probably, if the truth were known, pride of ownership and the joy of working with a superbly crafted tool is the most common reason. But, beyond that, there are advantages to each of the super-vises.

A Porsche is more fun to drive than a Ford and will get you where you are going considerably faster. So, too, with one of these vises, they are more pleasant to use simply because they are handcrafted and reflect that background in smoother operation, nicer finishing, and more options. They get you where you are going faster because they are designed with features that speed up the tying process. For the commercial fly tyer that speeding up of the tying process may dictate the need for such a vise because, to him, time is money. But for the advanced tyer who is spending his time at the bench dressing flies for his own use, convenience, pride of ownership, and the visual and tactile pleasure of working with a fine tool are reasons enough to opt for that new Porsche of the fly-tying world.

The real top-of-the-line vises have several things in common with each other—not the least of which is cost. Just what are you getting for your money? We're going to take a good look at each of several models, but there are several features that are common to all of them, besides their cost.

Probably the most impressive thing about all of these vises is the workmanship used in their construction. Without exception they are all beautifully finished pieces of equipment. Another thing that they all have in common is the innovativeness of their design.

We found when talking and corresponding with the builders of the vises that none of them had set out with the concept of designing a vise for the purpose of marketing it. All of them simply set about building a vise for their own use with the features they felt were lacking in the vises commercially available. Each of the vises that we are going to discuss is still built, to some degree by hand.

Another thing common to all of the vises we are going to discuss is the warranty: Virtually all of these vises carry a lifetime guarantee, which covers anything other than deliberate abuse.

We have tied at least several dozen flies on each of these vises. In most cases, this was not enough to evaluate their durability, but keep in mind that they all carry a lifetime guarantee, which speaks pretty well for their ability to last. Every vise is superbly crafted, and we can, without exception, heartily recommend any of them for your tying bench.

There are a few models of vises in this price range that we didn't evaluate for one reason or another. Perhaps we already had some experience with one and couldn't in good faith recommend it. Maybe the manufacturer, for whatever reason, wouldn't lend us one to evaluate, or (most likely) the vise has come on the market since our study.

To put it simply, just because a particular model is not covered here does not mean that it isn't among the best around. If you will only compare it to these and judge it on that basis, you can evaluate it very quickly for yourself.

Keep in mind that regardless of the beauty, features, and utility of a particular model, it must hold a hook! And it must hold that hook solidly. This is the first—the very first—thing that you should consider when evaluating a vise. There are a couple of different methods that the manufacturers use for clamping the hook in the vise.

The most common method is a tapered collet. In this type of construction, the rear shoulder of the jaw assembly is tapered and is fit inside a similarly tapered sleeve. As the jaw assembly is drawn back inside the sleeve the jaws are squeezed shut. Either of two methods may be used to draw the jaw assembly into the sleeve: a cam-shaped lever or a screw attached to the rear of the jaws. Which is best is a moot point, but both types have their strong advocates.

The proponent of the cam type will insist that this is the faster method (does a tenth-of-a-second difference in time to mount the hook really count?) and that it gives a more positive lock on the hook. The knob twisters, on the other hand, will be quick to remind you that a lever-cam type of vise requires adjustments in the vise for different hook sizes because the amount of drawing action is limited by the size of the cam. They will also tell horror tales of having to use several different-sized jaws to hold the full range of hooks (changing jaws is only a two-minute job), as if you switched from tying 4/0 hooks to #20s every time you sat down at the bench.

The truth is that it doesn't really matter. What does count is that, whichever method is used, the vise *holds* the hook and there are vises of each type that do the job superbly and there are some of each type that fail utterly. Once you have found a vise that performs the holding operation, then you have some choices to make as to type of base, finish, and particular features that are of importance to *you, you* . . . that's the key to the whole thing, you're not buying this vise for your tying instructor, your buddy, or us. Get the one that suits your style and feel of tying.

There are two base types that you may choose from: the pedestal base and the clamp type. The pedestal-base style has a large, heavy, metal base that sits on the tying bench. The prime advantage to the pedestal is that you can use it anywhere. The disadvantage is that, regardless of the weight of the base, within reason, it just doesn't provide for as steady a vise as the clamp type.

The clamp type has a clamp (much like a C-clamp) that attaches to the edge of a table and holds the vise post. This arrangement provides for a very solid mounting (limited only by the sturdiness of the table), allows you to vary the height of the vise, and also lets you rotate the vise towards or away from you. The disadvantage is that you must have a table with the right thickness of edge available to attach it to, although this disadvantage has been overcome in several models. Some manufacturers offer their vises with either type of base, and some are even interchangeable between a pedestal base and a clamp base.

One of the features that is common only in the top-of-the-line models is a choice of finishes. Nearly all of these vises are available with a black finish. If you spend long hours at the tying bench, the glare reflected from a shiny, chromed vise is very tiring to the eyes; the black finishes are meant to reduce this problem. The finishes used are either blueing, as seen on guns, or black chrome. Blued finishes are subject to rust, particularly where the hands are in contact with the surface. Vises with this finish do require some care, an occasional wiping down with light oil takes care of the problem, but it must be done! Black chrome suffers less from the problem of rust and is a truly beautiful finish. The disadvantages of the black-chrome finish is, first of all, the increased cost. To black-chrome metal requires a perfectly polished surface, which adds considerable time to the manufacturing process, and the chroming process is expensive in itself. Another catch is that the black-chrome finish is so smooth and shiny that it reflects nearly as much glare as a bright chrome finish, somewhat diluting the reason that a black finish was chosen to start with.

A bright chrome finish is standard on some of the models and probably is fine for anyone who doesn't spend long hours tying. It is an attractive finish and resists rust well without requiring much care. Another alternative that is available in a few models is a soft, or brushed, chrome finish. It offers an improvement as far as the glare problem, isn't any more expensive than bright chrome, and still resists rust well.

Now comes the tough part in deciding which vise to buy: Which one offers the features that are of the most importance to you? To help with the decision making, we will take a look at each of these selected vises and describe its particular attributes.

Thompson Pro II vise

Thompson Pro II. For those of us who started accumulating our tying hours on the old standby, the Thompson Model A, this vise from the same great company may be just the ticket. In essence, it is a Model A dressed up for the advanced (hence, "Pro") tyer. It lacks some of the features of the most expensive models, but then that becomes a matter of just what you consider worth paying for, doesn't it?

The Pro II is a simple, straightforward, honest, tying vise, and one with which any tyer could be pleased. In keeping with its intended role as a vise for the serious tyer, it is finished in black, which in this case is a blued finish (blueing is the name of the process, it really is black).

The vise is only available with a pedestal base. The base is well designed and heavy enough to provide a solid tying station. Unlike some of the pedestal vises that we've seen, the post on this one is short enough to allow you to use it on a normal-height desk or table without problems, while still allowing table clearance for the tying operation.

The vise comes with three sets of interchangeable jaws so that all sizes of hooks can be properly held. If you only tie on hooks larger than #18s and smaller than 1/0s, you can get by without the midge and super jaws and save some money.

The thing that most impressed us about the Pro II was the quality of workmanship evident in it. It is, of course, of a proven design (the A has been around for over 50 years now); as mentioned before, the pedestal/post is properly sized; it is very nicely finished; and it is as smooth working as a champion roping team. That there is a lot of hand workmanship used in the manufacturing process is evident. The Pro II carries an unconditional lifetime guarantee.

Price Vise. This vise is the brainchild of Eric Price of LaPine, Oregon. It is a knob-operated, collet type and will hold anything from a #8/0 saltwater streamer to a #32 without changing the jaws or adjusting the collet. It is finished in black, using a blueing process. The Price Vise is only available with a clamp base but the base is one of the best features of the vise: It will adjust for any table thickness up to 3¾". This eliminates the biggest drawback to a clamp-type base.

The vise is designed so that the hook can be pivoted up and down through a range from horizontal to about 85°, allowing the tyer to adjust the angle of the hook without removing it from the vise. It also allows you to set the jaws near vertical so that you can get to those really small hooks easier. Another feature is that the vise can be rotated 360° in the horizontal plane which is a nice advantage when you need to divide wings on dry flies. By rotating the hook so that the eye is facing you, it is much easier to get the wings divided equally.

Price vise

Probably the handiest feature of all, though, is that the hook can be rotated 360° on its own axis. This makes tying in a throat or beard hackle a snap since there is no need to remove the hook from the vise to turn it over to get underneath. It also makes the job of applying head cement easier. The jaws are rotated by pushing forward on the rear knob (the same one used to tighten the jaws) and then turning the whole collet assembly as desired. There is a positive lock at 180° and 360° which is set by simply allowing the knob to come back out to its original position.

This is the vise that we both have used for the past five years, and we can attest to its durability. A friend of ours, Hobie Ragland, is a commercial tyer and has used the Price Vise for years now. Hobie says that they will wear out—after about 2000 *dozen* flies. He should know, he's on his third one now!

If you think 2000 dozen won't get you through your remaining years, don't worry because the Price Vise carries a lifetime warranty.

The only accessory available for the vise with the base, is the unique light that attaches to the same clamp base as the vise. The light is flexible so that you can position as you desire, and it also includes a built-in magnifier.

Renzetti Presentation Vise. If your taste runs to something different, the Renzetti will catch your eye. This vise is a good example of the innovativeness of the designers of these super-vises. Basically the design is of the knob-operated collet type but that is where any resemblance to a "normal" vise ends. The head assembly appears to be upside down, but this was done for a very good reason as we'll see in a moment.

The vise comes equipped with jaws for size #2 to #16 hooks. Two additional sets of jaws can be bought, one to cover the range from #1 to 5/0, and another for hooks from #18 to #28. The changeover from one size to another takes less than a minute. The vise is available with a clamp-type base at a higher price than the Thompson and Price models.

The vise is designed so that you can rotate the hook through a full 360°

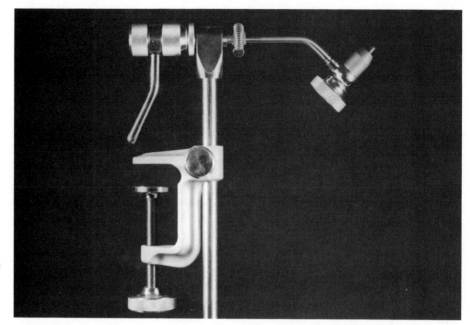

Renzetti Presentation vise

using an unusual and effective method: The lever at the rear of the vise is designed so that it will not rotate the vise when moved in one direction but will rotate the entire head assembly when moved the other way. This allows the tyer to rotate the vise to any point within the 360° movement, leave it there, and the hook is firmly in place at that position. The rotation feature is also one of the reasons for the unusual head position we mentioned earlier. If you were to clamp a hook in any vise and then rotate it, unless the hook was mounted perfectly parallel to the head assembly, the hook angle (from the horizontal plane) would change as the hook was rotated. By holding the hook from the bottom side, it will rotate on its own axis when rotated because the hook shank is aligned with the centerline of the head assembly. The only other way to overcome this problem is to build the vise so that the tyer can change the angle of the head after rotation. Also, since the hook will rotate without any eccentricity, you can wind materials on the hook by rotating the vise. The other reason for this head design is to give the tyer the maximum clear area around the hook, and it is one of the best features of the vise.

The Renzetti is one of the nicest finished vises that we have seen. It is constructed entirely of stainless steel, aluminum, and brass; therefore, rust simply isn't a problem. All of the metals are polished to the highest degree and the contrast between the brass and the stainless is most attractive. The vise comes equipped with a stainless-steel material clip. The Renzetti Presentation vise carries an unconditional, lifetime guarantee.

HMH Model Standard. The HMH is a lever-operated, collet-style vise of superb quality. For the most part, it is constructed of stainless steel. The cam-locking lever is of deep color, case-hardened carbon steel and the jaws are chrome moly tool steel. Each part of the vise is either machined from solid bar stock or investment cast and then machined and polished. This method of manufacture ensures that the vise is of the finest possible quality.

The vise is available in either a clamp mount or a pedestal base and will adapt to either type of mount. The pedestal base is absolutely gorgeous—solid polished brass. The clamp base has a wider opening than most we have seen (2½″) and will fit on most table edges. It comes equipped with two sets of jaws to cover the size range from 6/0 to #32. Two additional jaws are available as options, the Trout for sizes from #2 to #22, and the Restricted Use which has a very long thin set of jaws, for sizes #18 to #32. The Model Standard is only available in the polished finish. Since the vise is nearly entirely of stainless, it requires only an occasional wiping with light oil to remain in its pristine state.

The HMH will revolve in the horizontal plane so that you can look at the head or tail end of the fly which, as we mentioned earlier, is a real boon when dividing wings. The head can be angled up or down from horizontal to about 80° up. This is an important feature since the vise does allow the hook to be rotated 360°. The combination of these three modes of movement means that the hook will never need to be reset to accomplish any operation once it is clamped in the vise.

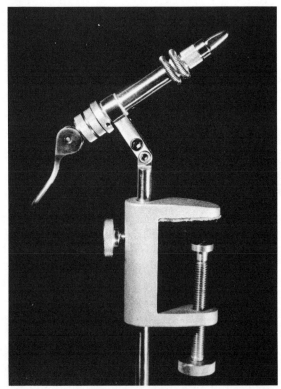

HMH Standard vise

This vise is a joy to tie on. It is smooth, solid, and entirely functional. The HMH was designed after a great deal of input from professional tyers and it really "does it all." It is used by many commercial tyers, which speaks well for the design and its durability. The Model Standard with two sets of jaws is in the most expensive range with the clamp base and even higher with the solid brass pedestal. Options include the alternate base, the Trout and Restricted Use jaws, and extra standrods. Each vise includes a stainless steel material clip.

The next two vises that we'll cover are both rather unique because each of them uses a method other than a tapered collet for clamping the vise jaws on the hook.

15

Xuron. The Xuron vise clamps the hook by means of a coarse-threaded screw that goes through one side of the jaw assembly and engages threads in the other side. When the lever attached to the screw is rotated, the two sides of the jaw are drawn together. This method is foolproof as the screw can be tightened to whatever point is needed to firmly anchor the hook. The only adjustment is that the lever can be inserted in any one of four holes in the shoulder of the screw so that the lever will be parallel to the vise body when the hook is properly clamped.

The Xuron is available in just about any configuration that the tyer might want: pedestal base, clamp base; black chrome, bright chrome, brushed chrome finish; and full rotating or non-rotating head. In keeping with its cost the vise is well finished and constructed of the finest materials.

The unusual shape of the standrod allows the tyer freer access to the hook and allows a slight amount of give to the vise which might act like a shock absorber, helping to avoid broken thread and slipping hackle pliers. The vise pivots by virtue of a ball-and-socket arrangement at the base of the standrod. This system, with the addition of the optional full rotary feature, allows movement of the vise in all planes. The tension of the pivot is simply adjusted by tightening or loosening a single thumbscrew.

The Xuron is a pleasant vise to use and, with the jaws tipped up, provides the most room when tying small flies that we've seen. It comes with a 90-day buy-back guarantee if you don't like it for any reason and, in addition, carries an unconditional guarantee, even to subsequent owners.

Xuron vise

Regal. The Regal vise looks a little strange and operates differently than any other vise we've seen, but when it comes to holding a hook, this beauty really shows its ability. The Regal works in the opposite mode from all of the other vises; instead of closing the jaws on the hook to anchor it, the jaws are permanently sprung closed. The jaws are forced open by means of a lever-operated cam, the hook inserted, and the jaws are allowed to close again. Unique—and effective!

The vise is available with a clamp or pedestal base and, in keeping with the rest of the design, this pedestal is different. The standrod is mounted in a vertical column so that the above-table height can be adjusted from about 7½″ to 9½″. This is an important feature since one of the problems in designing a pedestal-base vise is getting the standrod high enough to provide table clearance while still maintaining a comfortable working height.

The jaws and standrod are finished in black (blueing process), the balance of the vise is in an attractive gold/black pebble-grained finish.

The head of the vise is quite large, as this is the portion that holds the jaws sprung shut, but the jaws themselves are nicely shaped to allow plenty of working room around the hook. The head will pivot to the vertical position to provide additional room when tying small flies. One jaw has a slight notch cut on the inside that a large hook (#6 or larger) will fit into, providing an absolutely solid hold on the hook. One can put a 3/0 saltwater hook in the Regal and bend it into a complete circle, finally breaking it, without any hint of the hook slipping!

The Regal will hold any size hook, and with its pivoting head, even small sizes can be tied easily, but its real forte is in handling the larger sizes. For the individual who ties saltwater flies, large streamers, bass bugs, and the like, there simply is no finer vise and it will still handle the smaller, trout-sized hooks quite well.

Regal vise

Once we have made that all-important selection of a vise, we must make some decisions about the other tools that we'll need on the bench.

There are such an array of specialized tools available that it would be impossible for us to ferret out all of them, much less use each of them enough to really be able to give any solid comments. A gallows tool for tying parachute flies, hair-spinning tools, a separate thread clip, bobbin rests, wing formers, mirrors, and the like, are all pretty much designed for specific purposes and/or problems and just aren't used commonly enough to warrant coverage.

The makers of the tools we are going to discuss, Matarelli, Renzetti, J. D. (Dorin), and Thompson, each have their own ideas as to what makes each tool do its job better, but they all have one thing in common—quality! In some instances one of the manufacturers may have had a better idea than the rest on some minor point and, by the same turn, he may have been not quite as observant about a minor point on one of his tools. Any of these tools will do the job for which it was designed; we are simply going to try to point out the features of each. Nearly all of the companies mentioned are basically one-man operations with some occasional help to meet big orders. It really is a labor of love as most of the makers are former machinists who designed better tools for themselves and suddenly found themselves in business. Money is not the deciding factor, certainly.

I had a very long chat with Frank Matarelli, also with Don Dorin of J. D. Fly Tying Tool Co., and they both were quick to point out that their tools are entirely handmade. When you consider that the Matarelli bobbin requires over 40 hand operations, is made from stainless steel surgical tubing, and is not only functional but beautiful, it seems incredible that you can buy it for so little. The J. D. teardrop hackle pliers are made of spring steel, formed by hand, heat-treated, and the jaws are hand-lapped to ensure smooth edges—and the price is absurdly low. The Renzetti combination dubbing teaser and twister is made entirely of stainless steel and brass, shaped by hand and polished to perfection, at an easily affordable cost. Yes, it has to be a labor of love—these manufacturers are working too hard for their money.

In talking and corresponding with these gentlemen it was obvious that there was a friendly rivalry among them, but I got the feeling that it really didn't have much to do with the marketplace. Instead, it was a matter of pride to each that he was turning out the best possible tools. As long as that is the prevalent attitude, we fly tyers can only be grateful that a few men care so much. If you shop around, you can find most of these tools (imported) and save, perhaps, 50 to 75 cents; if so, that'll be the most expensive half-dollar that you never spent.

As with vises, the principal factor in selecting tools has to be, above all else, utility. No matter how well constructed, how innovative, or how nicely finished the tool is, if it doesn't accomplish efficiently the job for which it was designed, and it doesn't increase your pleasure at the tying bench, it isn't worth the space it occupies in the clutter.

SCISSORS

Scissors are the one tool that is absolutely indispensable to the fly dresser. The tyer who wants to upgrade his equipment is advised to make this his first purchase. Really, having an exceptionally good pair of scissors is certainly more important than having a "better" vise than the one you've been using. It is simply impossible to put together a neat, well-tied fly without having a good pair of scissors to work with.

There are several makes of fly-tying scissors on the market and some of them (Thompson, for one) are of pretty good quality, but I have noticed in looking through my library of fly-tying books that, although each of them mentions fly-tying scissors, fly-tying scissors are *not* what is shown in use in the book's illustrations. In the same vein, all of the fly-tying material catalogues show fly-tying scissors but you rarely see an accomplished tyer using them. Why? Well, because there are better scissors available, and the importance of good scissors is great enough for the advanced tyer to discover them. Invariably these better scissors come from the world of medicine. The surgeon requires the same qualities in his scissors as the fly tyer: fine points, smooth operation, and a really keen edge which stays that way.

You are probably already aware of it, but we'll cover it again, you need, *no,* absolutely *must* have, two pair of scissors for fly-tying; a heavy pair for cutting materials such as deer hair, tinsel, wire, latex, and other tough materials and a fine pair for cutting *only* thread, hackle, quill sections, and the

Scissors; left to right: corneal section scissors, tungsten scissors, curved Iris, bandage scissors, straight Iris, Dorin nippers

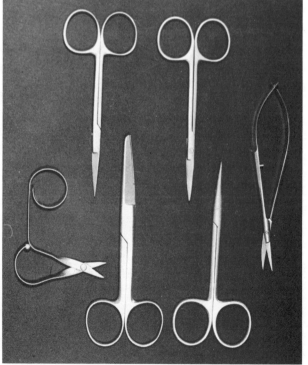

18

like. The heavy pair can be inexpensive although you should pay some attention to quality and size—they *do* have to cut and be usable in rather small areas. This heavy pair isn't too difficult to find. In fact, if you have been using your fine fly-tying scissors for cutting everything, why not delegate them to the role of "heavy" scissors since they're probably ruined anyway? The best heavy scissors we have found are the ones illustrated here. They are also medical scissors but, as you can see from the photo, they are much sturdier than the fine scissors shown. They are called bandage scissors. Their only drawback is that they are expensive, but they really stand up to the demands of the serious fly tyer. Choosing and purchasing a pair of really good fine scissors is much more difficult.

Probably the most popular scissors are called Iris scissors in the medical world. They are available with either straight or curved blades, are made entirely of stainless steel, retain their edge well and are fairly expensive. We both have several pair and the first ones bought are now about ten years old, aside from the fact that they are a little smoother working than the newer ones, it is almost impossible to tell them apart. They are only deficient in two areas: the size of the finger holes and the fact that one of the blades is a little thicker than the other. The finger holes are large enough for all but those people who really have large hands. The other point, one blade being a little thicker than the other, is a bit annoying. Since it is necessary to trim materials off as close to the hook as possible, your blade determines how close you can cut. With one very thin blade and another that is not quite so thin, you can hold the scissors to either trim close on the top side of the fly or on the under side—but not both. This means that you have to turn the scissors over in your hand occasionally or go through some real gyrations to get the thin side of the scissors where you need it. It quickly becomes habit, but it would be great if someone would make identical scissors with *both* blades thin.

What may be the finest of the fine scissors are called corneal section scissors and are used by eye surgeons for corneal transplants. We mentioned these in our first book and have been surprised that none of the fly-tying suppliers picked up on it and offered them to their customers. To the best of our knowledge they are only available through medical supply houses and they are *extremely* expensive. Don't misunderstand, we're not saying that they are necessary, but they are a real luxury when tying small flies.

They take some getting used to since they have no finger holes but Don ties with them most of the time and has learned to keep them in his hand all the time. He simply holds them with the tips up in the web between his thumb and first finger and since the blades are always open (because of the spring handles) there's no need to change the scissor's position to use them.

I don't use mine nearly as much as Don but when I start tying flies down in the sizes of below #18 or so, I get them out. They are also the very best tool I've seen for shaping spun hair, especially on flies like Goddard Caddis, Irresistibles, and Muddler Minnows in small sizes.

Hunter's, of New Boston, New Hampshire, offers what is absolutely the best pair of scissors we have ever seen. We spotted them in his catalogue and wrote Bill, asking him to send us a pair to look at—they are outstanding!

At first glance these scissors seem to be just another pair of Iris scissors, but with gold-plated handles. They are of stainless steel but with one very important difference: The blades are made with tungsten-carbide cutting edges inletted into the stainless! Tungsten carbide is one of the hardest metals known to man, so hard, in fact, that it can only be worked with diamond-cutting tools. These scissors are not only incredibly sharp, they will stay that way! In his catalogue, Bill says that Lefty Kreh has a pair he has been using for eight years that have never been resharpened. The manufacturer guarantees their keeping an edge for two years, and if they should dull after that, they will resharpen them for a small fee and guarantee them for another two years.

In addition to being so sharp, and so durable, they are absolutely the smoothest scissors we have ever seen. The ones that Hunter's sell are what the manufacturer calls "cosmetic rejects"; they are functionally perfect but the gold plating on the handles is smudged or has a slight scratch. That cosmetic flaw means that you can buy them for about thirty dollars less than the surgeon will pay for a "perfect" pair. They come in either straight or curved blade models. The curved-blade model is a little less than the straight-blade model.

As great as they are, they do have a few drawbacks. Like the Iris scissors, one blade is slightly thicker than the other, but, as we said, this is not a serious concern, however. Because the tungsten carbide is so hard, it will break! Drop them on a hard floor or catch the point in the eye when trimming close, give a little twist, and the tips are broken. If you forget or are in a hurry and use them to cut off a piece of ribbing wire the odds are, you will break a piece out of the edge. Try not to find out! In any event, however, the manufacturer can usually regrind the points for you for a small fee. The other problem, Bill says, is that they have a nasty way of disappearing when used at crowded tying functions.

Certainly not in the same category as the Hunter Tungsten Carbide scissor but very interesting and usable are the Dorin Nippers from the J. D. Fly Tying Tool Company. These are a well-thought-out tool designed specifically for the fly tyer. They are made of tempered spring steel, are very sharp, and, really, quite handy. The unique thing about them is that they are designed to be "worn" by the fly tyer. They have an adjustable ring that fits over the middle finger of the bobbin hand and the points of the scissors rest against the upper side of the index finger. They are out of the way when tying but are instantly ready to be used. The blades are spring-loaded to the open position so that only the thumb is needed to actuate the cutting action.

These are not meant to completely replace your scissors as you will still need your scissors for cutting and preparing material, trimming deer-hair bodies, and other such tasks. They are really great for the on-the-hook work during the tying operation though. If your budget is limited, we recommend these as a good, usable tool until you can move up to something better.

BOBBINS

The bobbin has a number of uses for the fly tyer. The principal one is that the bobbin, by its weight, provides enough tension on the thread to keep everything in place during the tying process. Those who are new to the world of fly-tying and have always tied with a bobbin rarely appreciate just what a boon that is. Before bobbins were popular, you finished each step of the tying process with a couple of half-hitches so that your hands could be free for handling materials. This not only slowed the tying process down considerably, it often resulted in flies that weren't as durable as you might like. If you have ever used half-hitches, you know how quickly that knot loosens, and if the tyer wasn't careful, some of the materials wouldn't be bound too tight. One way to avoid this problem was to keep adding some sort of cement to the fly as each section was tied. This resulted in a very durable fly but, of course, also added additional weight. The bobbin overcomes all of these problems and one other big one.

When tying without a bobbin, the tying thread must pass through the fingers and if your fingers aren't as smooth as "a schoolmarm's leg," the thread becomes frayed. The bobbin eliminates this by allowing the tyer to control the thread's position and tension, without handling the thread itself.

You will still occasionally see a tyer who ties without a bobbin and occasionally someone who is using a Chase or S & M bobbin, but the spring-wire types have just about taken over the market. They are simple, efficient, and inexpensive. Since there are no moving parts, there is nothing to lose or get maladjusted, and because the spool becomes, in essence, a part of the tool, you have an easy means of adjusting tension while tying by simply closing the hand tighter around the spool.

On all of the bobbins of this type, the only adjustment that you can make is the tension that the legs apply to the spool, and this is done simply by springing them further apart or closer together. The tension should be set so that the thread will come off the spool easily and yet tight enough that the spool won't unwind from the weight of the bobbin.

All of the fly-tying tool companies make this style of bobbin, and, essentially, they are pretty much the same, but, as with all of the tools, there are minor differences that the manufacturer felt were worthwhile.

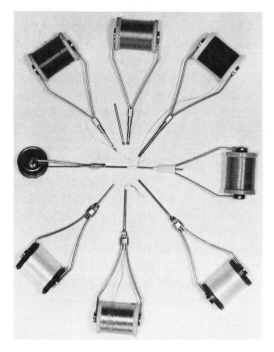

Bobbins; clockwise from top: Matarelli, Matarelli, Matarelli, Dorin, Dorin, Dorin, Renzetti, Matarelli

All of the bobbins that we are going to look at are of good quality, and you're not likely to have any problems with any of them. There are, however, some cheap models around that can cause you some grief; so here are a few things to look for. Chromed bobbins are prone to cutting the tying thread because the plating eventually chips around the tip of the tube, leaving a razor-sharp edge. The spool buttons must be firmly attached to the spring wires or they will come loose and then the spool won't stay aligned with the thread tube. The bobbins we will talk about are all available at a moderate cost. At most, you might be able to buy something else and save a dollar. It probably isn't going to be worth it!

To the best of our knowledge, the Matarelli was the first bobbin of this type. Frank Matarelli designed and built the first ones in 1954 and his Standard bobbin has remained pretty much the same ever since. Its design is so clean and efficient that it has been copied by nearly every tying tool company in the world. Frank makes his bobbins in five styles now: the Standard, the Standard with a longer tube, the Midge, the Midge with a longer tube, and the Material bobbin, which has a flared end for handling floss and materials other than thread.

The Standard model comes in your choice of a long-tube (1½″ tube length) or short-tube model (¾″ tube length). Which tube length you should choose is purely a matter of personal choice. Some people make a claim for "better thread control" for the long-tube type, but I fail to see where you have better control when the end of the tube is further from the controlling source—your hand. I don't think there is a good argument for either style over the other; I prefer the short-tube and Don likes the long-tube model better but I'd be hard pressed to defend my choice.

Frank's Midge bobbin is a real dream to work with. It is considerably smaller than the Standard primarily because it doesn't use the original thread spool. Instead, you transfer the thread to a sewing-machine bobbin. The tube diameter is slightly smaller than on the Standard so some additional weight is saved also. When you are tying the really small flies, this reduction in weight is important because the wire used for the hook is so fine that a regular-weight bobbin may bend the hook.

The disadvantage, of course, is that you have to transfer the thread to the smaller spool, but that is easily accomplished if you make sure that you buy bobbins that fit the family sewing machine. You don't even have to bother with that, a bolt with a nut to hold the bobbin against the bolt head, chucked in an electric drill allows you to transfer the thread in about 20 seconds!

Ah, but there are advantages other than reduced weight! The spring-wire bobbins were really great and then the thread manufacturers started getting cheap. First, they replaced the nicely finished wooden spools, which worked so well in our bobbins, with plastic spools. These plastic spools simply aren't as smoothly finished around the center hole and just don't fit the bobbin buttons as well. They also always seem to have little pieces of plastic that extend from the rim of the spool which have an affinity for catching the tying thread. Now we are starting to see plastic foam spools and this miserable stuff provides a lot of friction and, in addition, is very soft and easily damaged by the button ends.

The metal sewing-machine bobbins are perfectly smooth, both around the center hole and around the rim. Any particular size that you pick will always be exactly that same size and as long as you stay with that size, you will never need to adjust the tying-bobbin's legs. Another advantage is size; one of the sewing-machine bobbins will easily hold a full 200-yard spool of thread and yet is only one-fourth as thick. That means that you can store the same number of spools in one-fourth the space. There is the additional cost of purchasing the sewing-machine bobbins to think about, but they are quite cheap and frequently can be picked up on sale.

The Matarelli Midge bobbin is available with either the long or short tube. The other bobbin, which Matarelli offers, is called a Material bobbin and is meant for use with floss and other materials besides thread. The tip of this model is machined with a flare in the end of the tube so that floss can flatten out as it is wrapped on the hook.

The Matarelli line of bobbins are all constructed of stainless steel of the same type used for hypodermic needles. They are beautifully made and finished. Of particular importance is the fact that the inside of the tube ends are polished perfectly smooth so that there is no danger of cutting tying thread. Frank's bobbins originally set the standard for the industry and, although there are others that are of as good quality, there are none that are any better.

Renzetti offers four styles of bobbins, all of the spring-wire type. All four of the bobbins are constructed of stainless steel and brass. The Renzetti bobbins are well finished, including that most important point of getting the end of the thread tube perfectly smooth to avoid cutting the tying thread. Two of the models are designed to be used for other than thread; these two have large plastic balls instead of brass spool buttons. This was done because tinsel and floss often come now on plastic foam spools and the larger buttons hold these spools without smashing them.

The bobbin illustrated here is the Midge Model A. It is a neat, lightweight, little bobbin meant for tying smaller flies. This particular model was appealing because it has a short tube (½″), which just seems to make it handier when working on the really small sizes.

Also in the line is a model called the Streamer bobbin. Actually, it is what we would probably consider a standard-sized, long-tube bobbin. It is a little larger and, of course, a little heavier than the Midge. Like the Midge, this model has the standard brass spool buttons.

There are two special bobbins available: One for lead wire and tinsel and one meant for floss. Both of these use the large plastic balls as spool buttons. The lead wire and tinsel bobbin is about the same size as the Streamer bobbin but has a larger diameter tube to handle the heavier material. The floss bobbin also has a larger tube than the Streamer model and, in addition, the end of the tube is flared so that the floss can spread out as it is wrapped.

J. Dorin (J. D. Fly Tying Co.) makes three different models of bobbins. At first glance they appear to be like other spring-wire bobbins, but on closer examination there is a difference! Instead of the tying thread passing through the length of the thread tube, there is a slot milled in the side of the tube just above the tip and the thread passes down the *outside* of the tube, enters the slot, and then goes through only about ³⁄₁₆″ of the tube and out the end. This innovative approach has a couple of advantages to the tyer. First of all, since most tyers use waxed tying thread, you don't have the problem of the tube getting filled with wax. Secondly, the bobbin is very easy to thread since you only have to get the thread through that last little section of the tube. Additionally, with the thread on the outside of the bobbin tube, it is directly under your finger and this gives an additional means of controlling thread tension.

The Dorin bobbins are available in a long-tube model, called the Maxi, and in a short-tube, lighter-weight model called the Classic. They also have a neat style called a Dual that is either a short- or a long-tube model at the tyer's whim. This is achieved by sliding an extra tip section inside of the short tube to add about a half-inch to the tube length.

All of the bobbins are constructed of stainless steel and brass. They are well finished and the tubes are smoothly polished to avoid any problems with cutting thread.

HACKLE PLIERS

In our first book, we said that the best hackle pliers we had found still slipped sometimes and occasionally cut the hackle. This is still true but there have been some new approaches to the problem of holding a delicate feather so that it can be wrapped around the hook and things have improved.

We'll break the available types down as follows: English style, Duplex style, and others. The English style are made of spring wire and have overlapping tips made by flattening the wire. They are available in several sizes and have always seemed to work better for us than the Duplex type.

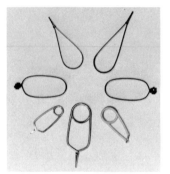

Hackle pliers; clockwise from top: Dorin Tear Drop, Thompson Duplex, Dorin J model, English style, English style, Thompson Non-Skid, Dorin Tear Drop

The Duplex type of hackle pliers are made of flat spring steel with pads attached to the overlapping ends. These pads may be both of metal (often serrated), one metal and one rubber, or both of rubber. On the ones with one or both pads of rubber, the rubber eventually hardens, and then they don't work. Occasionally, the rubber pads, if left together, stick to one another, and then they are ruined. However, there are a lot of very good fly tyers who prefer the Duplex style to the English style. The Duplex simply works better for them! The whole point is that you must find the tools that work best for you and your style of tying; don't be too dependent on what someone else thinks. You might find that one of the new, non-traditional, types works best on your tying bench.

The new hackle pliers are from the J. Dorin line and, frankly, we think they are much better than the older types. We'll talk more about that later.

The Thompson Company markets a complete line of hackle pliers that includes two duplex types and two sizes of English styles. One of their duplex styles is called a Duplex and has one pad of serrated brass and the other of rubber. The other style is called Non-Skid and they have both pads of rubber. Both of these pliers are well made with good spring tension and well-aligned jaws.

The English styles that they make are identical except for the size. They call the larger size English Hackle Pliers and the smaller one Midget Hackle Pliers. The English style of pliers seems to hold the hackle with less problem of slippage than the Duplex, and I suspect this is because the English styles have a larger bearing surface on the hackle. On the other hand, they are much more likely to cut the hackle. For the English style to work well, they have to fit perfectly so that the jaws are evenly mated for their entire length. The only way to keep them from cutting the hackle is to smooth the edges so there is nothing to cut with. These two qualities, when present, make a hackle plier that is efficient and pleasant to use. It requires some handwork to arrive at that point, and it is obvious that the Thompson Pliers have been mated and finished by hand so that they do work well. Their Midget model is particularly nice to use, not only for small flies, but for all your tying.

J. Dorin set out to find a better system and just may have succeeded. They make two different types of pliers, both of which are unique.

Their J model is made from a coiled piece of tempered, heavy, music wire with one end bent to hook over the other. All but the hooked end is sheathed with plastic tubing. When the tip of the hackle is fastened between the hook and the plastic-coated end, the hackle simply will not pull out, in fact, the hackle will break before it slips. Since all of the gripping surfaces are round, there is nothing to cut the hackle, either. The only drawbacks to the J model are that it uses a little larger portion of the hackle to clamp than the traditional styles, which is a problem if tying small flies, and they don't allow the tyer to wrap the hackle by putting a finger in the loop at the end and winding it on.

They also make two sizes of what they call the Tear Drop hackle pliers. These are made of flat spring steel but the ends don't overlap. Instead, the two ends are loosely riveted together, just behind the tip. This means that the tips are always pressed together and when you attach them to a hackle, they really hold. They come in two sizes, 2.5 grams and 5 grams. The tips come to a small point so holding a small hackle is no problem. Another feature is that the jaws open very easily, which is important when teaching a youngster to tie. I've noticed that a lot of the tyers in the booths at shows are using this new hackle plier and I think that speaks well for the design.

There are some other companies that make hackle pliers and some of them are quite good, too. Again, the things to look for are smooth edges and perfectly mated jaws. If you should get a pair of English-style hackle pliers that just don't work right, you can probably correct the problem by doing the handwork that the manufacturer didn't take care of. Double a piece of fine emery paper, place it between the closed jaws and work it back and forth. Make sure that you also work it over the edges so that they become slightly rounded. When the jaws are nicely mated and the edges rounded, replace the emery paper with crocus cloth and repeat the process. When you get them lapped and polished they will really work well, and you'll wonder how the manufacturers can sell the things for so little.

WHIP FINISHERS

We have often said that if you really want to get an argument raging among fly tyers, all you need to do is bring up the subject of whip finishers. We wrote an article for *Flyfishing the West* magazine on how to tie the whip finish without using a tool and were upbraided both in a letter to the editor and a personal letter about the disservice that we were doing the fly tyer by making him believe that you needed to know how to tie the knot by hand. The individual (who just happens to make whip finishers, by the way) argued that since the whip finish is such a difficult knot to tie, it was shameful to discourage the use of a tool to make the job easier, and I guess that is a valid point. Or, as another manufacturer put it, "You wouldn't think of advocating that the tyer get by without a vise or bobbin, and yet you can tie a fly without either tool . . . why pick on the whip finisher?" Again that sounds like a valid argument. But both of these gentlemen have overlooked a couple of points.

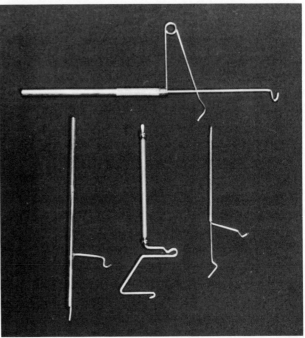

Whip finishers; top: Thompson; bottom, left to right: Charlie's Whipper (large), Matarelli, Charlie's Whipper (small)

The argument that the whip-finish knot is hard to tie only perpetuates the idea, it is *not* hard to tie the whip finish by hand! We have taught several thousand people from age seven or eight to seventy or eighty to accomplish the task. It's a lot easier than tying a barrel knot to attach a new tippet section to your leader, for example. We certainly wouldn't advocate tying flies without a vise or bobbin, but the assembling of a fly is an involved process, much more so than the simple matter of tying a single knot. Finally, we have never held that the tyer shouldn't use a whip finisher. On the contrary, we have pointed out all along that many excellent tyers do use one; all that we have said is that the tyer should know how to tie the knot by hand so that he isn't completely debilitated if he finds that the whip finisher is home on the tying bench and he has all of the other materials he needs to cash in on a trout-feeding spree. We still hold to that philosophy.

Whip finishers come in, basically, two styles. The first style has a head assembly made of spring wire, whereas the second type is made of very heavy, rigid wire. They work equally well but most tyers seem to prefer the rigid type.

Renzetti and Thompson make the spring-wire styles while Matarelli and Charlie Cole (Charlie's Whipper) make the rigid type. All four of the manufacturers turn out well-finished whip finishers, and we would be hard pressed to pick one over the other.

Charlie's Whipper is available in two sizes while Matarelli has only one size. It really doesn't appear that there is a need for different sizes as far as finishing the fly goes, it is more a matter of providing the tyer with a choice as to what feels best to him.

Thompson makes their spring-wire type in two sizes and the Renzetti is only available in one size.

Since I haven't used a whip finisher in years, testing the available makes also involved relearning how to use them. Charlie's Whipper seemed the easiest to learn to use, the Matarelli just about ties the knot by itself, once you've caught the knack of it. Like most tyers we've met who use the whip finisher, I much prefer the rigid type to the spring-wire styles, although they, too, are relatively easy to use.

After learning, again, to use the whip-finishing tool, I tied several dozen flies using both types. I got so that I was pretty quick with them and they really do make tying the knot quick and easy. You might want to consider one of these if you still have trouble with the whip finish. As for me, well, I can still do it faster, easier, and with better control by hand.

OTHER TOOLS

There are many other tools made for the fly tyer. Some of these might well be considered by all tyers whereas some of them are designed only for very special purposes. Additionally, some of the tools (hackle guards, for instance) are meant for the beginning tyer who might be having problems with a particular step in the tying process. The advanced tyer is not likely to be interested in such tools so we will limit our discussion to tools in the first two categories: Those that may be of benefit to all tyers and the special-purpose tools that are available for special tasks.

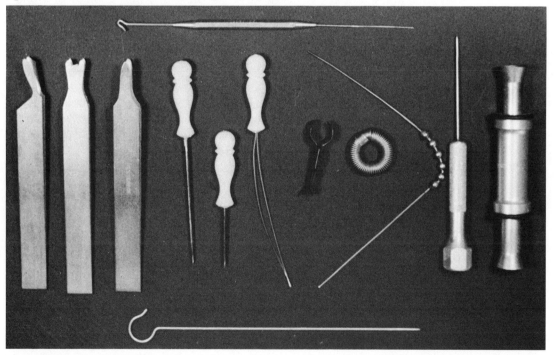

Miscellaneous tools; top: Renzetti dubbing twister/teaser; center, left to right: Renzetti wing formers, Dorin bodkins, Dorin bobbin threader, Thompson material clip, Dorin material clip, Matarelli bobbin threader/cleaner, Thompson bodkin, Renzetti hair stacker; bottom: Matarelli dubbing twister/bodkin

One of the most usable auxiliary tools is a material clip. This is a small device that attaches on the shank of the vise behind the head and is used to hold tied-in materials out of the way until they are ready to be used.

They are available in two types: Thompson makes one that snaps onto the vise with a single vertical clip, and J. Dorin manufactures theirs from a spring which fits completely around the vise shank, the HMH and Renzetti vises come equipped with this type.

At first glance it would seem that the spring type is superior because the spaces between the windings of the spring provide a lot more places to hold your materials. The clip type, however, works just as well since we tie all of our materials in the reverse order that they are going to be used. So even though the materials are stacked one on top of the other, the material that you need is always on top and accessible.

The only disadvantage to the spring type is that most of them are made with the two ends on the spring bent into hooks and hooked together. This leaves some little hooks sticking out that easily catch the thread and the tied-in materials. The J. Dorin is made with one end of the spring tapered so that it fits inside of the other, leaving a perfectly smooth junction.

A material clip is a very inexpensive addition to your tying bench. If you tie a lot of streamers, steelhead flies, or salmon flies where you often tie in several body materials, ribbing, and the like; then a material clip will really be useful.

A bodkin (or dubbing needle, as it is sometimes called) is almost a necessity. It is used to section material such as quills, to pull out hackle fibers that have been caught under the tying thread, to fluff up dubbing, to apply head cement, and for a myriad of other tasks.

The simplest bodkin is just a large needle stuck into a piece of wood dowel, and you can make one for pennies. The ones that are on the market are fairly inexpensive, though, and many of them have some additional features that are worthwhile.

J. Dorin makes two sizes of bodkins, one with a 1¼″ needle and a larger one with a 2½″ needle. In both sizes, the needle is firmly mounted in an attractive plastic handle, and it is the handle that we feel is the drawback. It is round; and one of Fling's and Puterbaugh's maxims is that anything round will roll off the tying bench, or be otherwise out of reach, within 10 seconds of when you need it.

The Thompson bodkin is a beauty. It has a nice, large aluminum handle the end of which is hex shaped so that it can't roll. The 2″ needle is firmly attached in the handle and the round part of the handle is knurled for a sure grip.

Matarelli combined his bodkin and dubbing twister into one tool. It is in the shape of a shepherd's crook, about 5½″ long overall. This is a natural combination since one of the uses of the bodkin is to pick out the dubbing after it is applied to the hook. The Matarelli is made of heavy, stainless steel wire.

The Renzetti is fashioned of a small diameter, hex-shaped, brass rod. The combination of the brass handle and the stainless steel wire used for the needle makes this the most attractive bodkin we have seen.

There is really not much to recommend one of the styles over the others and the price is reasonable enough so that that isn't a consideration either.

Renzetti makes the neatest hair stacker that we have seen. The main body is made of aluminum with two different sizes of brass tubes that fit into either end. Each end of the main body has a rubber O-ring attached so that you won't wake the entire family when you start tapping it on the bench. You really do need two different sizes of stackers, one for short hair for use on small flies and another for longer hair for the big stuff and this tool gives you both. They also make two individual sizes, a large and small, but aside from the cost savings, it is more convenient to have both sizes available in one tool.

There are others on the market that are worth mentioning, although we don't have a picture of them. The Laggie's is a good one. Hunters offer two different models: One is made of solid rosewood (how's that for class?), and they also have an knurled aluminum model that is available in three sizes.

If you are into hairwing flies at all, a hair stacker is a real time-saver and will result in a better-looking fly.

Matarelli, Thompson, and Renzetti all make dubbing twisters. As we discussed, Matarelli combined his with his dubbing needle into one tool. The Thompson is a one-use tool, and the Renzetti makes a single-use tool and a combination dubbing twister and teaser that is really nice.

The Matarelli is the most efficient of them all simply because it is smaller in diameter. That's right, because the diameter is smaller, it will make more revolutions with each roll between your thumb and finger. It will twist the loop quicker, so that makes it more efficient, right?

The Renzetti has the same small, hex-shaped brass handle as their dubbing needle and is very nice looking. The combination tool has the dubbing twister on one end and the other end is a piece of stainless wire with very fine teeth cut into it for fluffing dubbing. Both ends work well, and it is quite cheap.

Since pre-waxed tying thread has become so popular everyone suffers from a chronic case of "clogged bobbin." Renzetti and Matarelli both offer tools to clean the wax out of the bobbin's thread tube.

The Matarelli is combined with another essential tool for the waxed-thread user: a bobbin threader. The bobbin threader is a loop of very fine spring wire that will reach clear through the tube so that you can insert the thread and pull it out the end. These two tools are joined with a short section of stainless bead chain so that it will fold to fit better in your tying box.

Renzetti also mates the two tools into one, although theirs has a solid body section of the same hex-shaped brass rod. They also make the two tools as individual items.

J. Dorin's has a somewhat better approach to the bobbin threader than the others. They make the fine wire loop with one "leg" slightly longer than the other so that when the loop is inserted in the bobbin tube, a small space is automatically formed making it easier to get the thread into the threader loop.

Renzetti makes a line of interesting, very usable tools that fall into the category of those that not everyone needs but that are indispensable to the tyers of certain types of flies. They are called Wing Formers and they are tweezer shaped pieces of flat brass stock whose ends are milled into the shape of wings and wing cases of common aquatic insects. To use these, you simply select a feather, insert it between the sides of the wing former and, with a match or lighter, burn the feather to the perfect shape and size needed.

They come in four sizes each for caddis wings, mayfly wings, wing cases for stonefly and mayfly nymphs, and jungle cock eyes. The sizes cover the complete range from hook size #10 to #20 for the dry-fly wings and #4 to #12 for wing cases. They are easy to use and eliminate the tedium of trying to cut a small feather to shape.

One of the most important tools on the tying bench is the light. It is simply impossible to tie for very long or to tie really good flies under poor lighting conditions. There are many different options that may be tried to achieve good lighting but nothing, nothing compares to the Price Vise Lamp.

The lamp was designed to be used with the Price Vise and will attach directly to the vise base so that the lamp takes up no table space, but it is also available as a separate unit with its own base so that you can have the advantages of the Price Lamp even if you choose to use another brand of vise.

Price Vise Lamp

The space-saving mounting system is only the first of the many advantages of the lamp. It is completely flexible so that the light can be positioned precisely as you need it quickly and easily. Mine has even been pulled over to shine on the floor under the vise more than once to find dropped items. The light uses a standard light bulb (inexpensive to replace, with a choice of light intensity provided just by changing the bulb), and is insulated so that the shade won't burn your fingers when touched. It has a superb magnifier attached that has a tremendous depth of field so that your hands, tools, and the fly aren't going in and out of focus as with most magnifiers. The magnifier is cleverly designed so that it swivels around the light and out of your way when not needed.

In short, it is the ultimate lighting system and, although it isn't cheap, it's worth every penny—and more!

Thompson has a neat device that is probably appreciated as much by the floor sweeper in the house as by the fly tyer. It is called a WasteTrol and is a small wire frame that attaches to the vise stem, under the bench, and holds a nylon bag open for all the little clippings of thread, hair, and other materials that accumulate during the tying session.

A worthwhile, inexpensive tool is a section cut from a sheet of plastic foam insulating material laid on the tying bench. Holes are easily cut in the material to hold bottles of head cement and paint, and small strips can be glued on top where you can stick your flies to dry. It also makes a great tool holder; just stick your bobbins, bodkins, scissors, and other tools into the soft material. Al Price discovered this trick, and it really adds to the efficiency of the tying area.

There are also some tools that fall into the luxury category. These are the ones that cost a lot and aren't really a necessity on the tying bench.

One of these is a fur blender. In fact, these are just miniature versions of the blender you probably have in the kitchen. For some tyers, who really mix large quantities of dubbing, it may be more than a luxury, but for most of us, twenty-five or thirty dollars for a device to simply mix fur together is a luxury.

I guess Hunter's tungsten carbide scissors would have to be considered a luxury at their price, but they are sure to add enjoyment to the time spent tying flies.

When it comes to pure, unadulterated, frivolous luxury I think that the fly-tying chest offered by Price Vise has got to be at the top of the list. Actually it is designed as a machinist's chest but Al and Eric have had some minor modifications made to improve it for the fly tyer.

These "tying chests" are constructed entirely of solid oak or walnut (your choice); they have a deep top compartment, two shallow, half-width drawers; two shallow, full-width drawers; and a deep, full-width drawer on the bottom. All of the drawers are made with dovetailed joints, are felt lined,

Price tying chest

and each is hand fitted to the chest. The Prices also provide a large assortment of small engraved labels so that you can mark the drawers as you wish. The quality of materials and the workmanship evident in these chests are reminiscent of turn-of-the-century craftmanship.

Luxury? You bet! There isn't any way that anyone can justify needing such an expensive addition to his tying bench. No, I can't justify it and don't have one but, well just maybe, someday. . .!

two
Hackle

We all know what a hackle is, right? Well, I thought I did until I sat down to try to fit a description to it. Now I can see why the beginner in the fly-tying game gets all confused; it is perplexing! The dictionary is the logical place to find a good definition so that was the first stop.

Webster defines hackle as: "one of the long, narrow feathers on the neck or saddle of a bird," and as: "the neck plumage of the male domestic fowl." Both of these seem to fit the fly tyer's idea of what a hackle is, however, when you start reading books on fly patterns you will find reference to such things as partridge, grouse, peacock, and snipe. The feathers from these birds certainly don't fit the second definition of: "the neck plumage of the male domestic fowl," and because the suggested feathers from these birds are body feathers, they don't fit the description about "long, narrow feathers on the neck or saddle of a bird" either.

The best we can do is to accept that when we speak normally of hackle, we are talking about the feathers from the neck or saddle of a rooster. We have to expand that definition to include feathers from the neck of a hen in some cases. And expand the definition even further to accept that, in a few cases, any feather that is used in the manner of a hackle is also called by that name.

Most fly tyers buy their hackle "on the skin," that is, the feathers are left attached to the neck or saddle skin of the bird. Those from the neck are called "necks," or "capes," while the ones from the rump are called "saddle patches."

We are going to limit our discussion to those hackles from the members of the chicken family, both rooster and hen. In talking about hackle there are three main areas that should be discussed: color, quality, and, of recently growing importance, commercially raised hackle.

COLOR

When we speak of hackle color, we are talking of the color of the individual feathers or hackles found on the neck. That is sometimes different from the overall color appearance of the neck. For example, you will sometimes find a brown neck that seems quite dark, but if you select an individual hackle from the neck, it will be several shades lighter than expected. Let's take a look now at hackle color, remembering that we are talking about the colors of the individual hackles.

White. White is a very common color in chickens, therefore, there are a lot of white necks around. The difficulty comes in finding a white neck of acceptable quality for dry flies; white hackle seems to run very soft. Fortunately, not many dry-fly patterns call for white hackle. For those occasional times when you do need a good white hackle, there is a solution.

If you have a splashed neck with some white hackles in it, they will nearly always be of the same quality as the basic-color hackles on the neck. Don't misunderstand, there are some white necks around with good dry-fly quality hackle, but they are rare and expensive. I recently saw a true white neck from one of Henry Hoffman's roosters that was as good dry-fly quality as any neck that I have ever seen, regardless of color. I still kick myself for not buying that one!

Cream. Cream hackle runs from just off-white to almost a honey color. A good, dry-fly quality, cream neck is not too hard to find. They are much more available than white and the really light ones will work as a substitute for white.

Ginger. Honey-colored hackle with just a touch of red to almost brown, are all in the range of ginger. To be a ginger, there has to be a tinge of red in the hackle. The shades of ginger are among the most used of all hackle. They are generally of good dry-fly quality and the medium-to-dark shades are not too expensive. Light ginger is relatively rare, and, it follows, considerably more costly.

Brown. The browns are the most popular colors. The color ranges from just darker than ginger to just short of black. Brown necks are the most available and the least expensive in dry-fly quality.

Coachman. Actually, coachman is just the darkest possible shade of brown. It isn't used much (the Royal Coachman fly is its namesake), and it's a good thing—they are quite rare in good quality.

Black. A true black is a rare find, most natural necks have a "dirty grey" cast that is hard to define, but very obvious. A true black neck is almost always of superb quality but you may never see one. If you do, it will almost certainly be a commercially raised one from the Metz Hatchery. Again, as we mentioned in regard to white hackles, you may find a splashed neck that contains a few black hackles and they will usually be of good quality. Black isn't often called for in fly-tying and, luckily, dyed black necks are usually of very good quality and are relatively inexpensive.

Dun. Webster defines dun as: "a variable color averaging a nearly neutral, slightly brownish, dark grey." That's a pretty good definition of a "medium-blue dun" for the fly tyer but we break the color down into some more specific categories. Light-blue dun is a pale shade of grey with bluish overtones; dark-blue dun is the color of blued steel. We then recognize those three basic dun colors that have additional shading. Bronze dun has a brownish cast, which gives it a bronze hue. Olive dun is a bronze dun with an almost imperceptible greenish tint. Iron-blue dun is one shade removed from black without any chalky appearance. The duns are the most sought after and the rarest of all the commonly called for hackle colors. Additionally, when one is found, it is usually of inferior quality—or, at least, that used to be the case. The Metz Hatchery of Belleville, Pennsylvania now raises natural dun birds by the thousands. Because the birds are raised specifically for fly-tying, they are bred to provide true dun colors, as well as for superb quality.

For the first time in the history of fly-tying, natural dun hackle is available to everyone. They aren't cheap, but, as we'll discuss later, considering the quality for the money, they aren't really expensive either.

Those are the basic colors of hackle. We then categorize them into other groups based on the markings.

Badger. A badger hackle is a white-to-ginger hackle with a dark center stripe. They are readily available and are usually of pretty good quality. A light badger is a good substitute when white is called for, as it is nearly always of better quality than a natural white.

Furnace. A dark ginger-to-coachman hackle with a dark center stripe is called a furnace. Furnace hackle is available in good dry-fly quality although, on the average, it is not of as good quality as the basic browns or badgers.

Cock-Y-Bondhu. This is a furnace hackle with the addition of dark tips on the edge of the feather (called a list). Cock-Y-Bondhu used to be called for in many patterns but, fortunately, that trend has passed. Most supply houses don't even list it as a specific type anymore and just include the ones they do get in with the furnace necks. Generally of about the same quality as the furnace necks.

Variants. By definition, a variant is a hackle having more than one color present. Usually a variant is thought of as a barred hackle. The variants are the most underused hackle in fly-tying.

Probably this is because it is very hard to define exactly what a given variant hackle looks like. Therefore, if a pattern called for a variant hackle, no one would be sure just what was needed. It is really unfortunate because variant hackle seems to almost always be of good quality and they have a breakup of color that lends a more natural appearance to our flies. Additionally, they are always of better quality for the money than any other hackle.

Splashed. These are the real weirdos among hackle. Splashed isn't really a hackle color, but rather a type of neck. Perhaps, "variant neck" would be a good definition. The hackles on the neck are each normally colored and marked but there will be individual feathers of two or three different colors on the neck. The most common is a brown neck with some white, and perhaps, a few black hackles present. This is the source for inexpensive but good-quality black-and-white feathers. Unfortunately, some suppliers have, in the last couple of years, started calling these necks variants, so be specific when ordering hackle. There is a difference between a variant hackle (a feather with more than one color present), and a variant neck (a neck with more than one color of hackle present). Caveat emptor!

There is one variant hackle that is so important to the fly tyer that it has acquired a name of its own: Grizzly. Grizzly is a black or grey hackle with white barring. Like the duns, grizzly necks in really good quality have always been expensive and difficult to obtain—no more!

Henry Hoffman, of Warrenton, Oregon, raises hundreds of roosters each year that are bred specifically for their hackle. They are absolutely gorgeous—perfectly shaped, heavily barbed, and beautifully marked. Like the Metz duns, they aren't cheap but are a good value.

Those are the basic colors and markings of hackle. There are others but if you can keep track of the ones we have discussed, you can satisfy 99% of the color requirements called for in fly patterns.

QUALITY

We all tend to think of good-quality hackle as hackle that has all the desirable traits for a dry fly; however, quality is a relative thing. The attributes that represent quality for a dry fly are exactly the opposite of what we would desire for a hackle to use on wet flies, nymphs, or streamers. I guess we all think of the dry-fly traits as representing quality because they are the rarer qualities in hackle.

I'll probably lapse into the same approach in our discussion of hackle quality but remember: When I describe a certain quality as being desirable in a neck or cape, I'm not implying that the lack of that quality makes the hackle worthless. On the contrary, the further away from my list of desirables that the hackle falls, the more usable it is on streamers, wet flies, and nymphs. When you get right down to it, probably the poorest hackle around is that which is not quite good enough for dry-fly use and too good for other uses.

Each color of hackle has a general quality that runs concurrent with that color. Basically, the quality of hackle declines as you move towards each end of the color spectrum. Both white and very dark brown tend to run soft, while the colors in the middle (ginger to medium brown) are more likely to be of good quality. That is not to say that there are no good white or coachman necks around, but they are much rarer in good, dry-fly quality than the middle shades. The typical quality of each hackle color was covered earlier.

To understand quality at either end of the scale, dry to wet, it is necessary to have a basic understanding of feather structure because each part of the feather has a bearing on whether the hackle is a good dry-fly hackle, good for wets, or one of those that isn't very good for either.

A feather is made up of three major parts. The shaft (or stem) of the feather is the heavy center part. The "branches" off the shaft are called barbs (sometimes flues). If you were to magnify one of these barbs, you would see smaller fibres extending out from each edge; these are called barbules. Now, let's see how each part of the feather affects the overall quality of the hackle.

Shaft. First of all, the shaft length is important because we want a feather long enough so that it can be wrapped several times around the hook shank.

If it is long enough, we will be able to hackle our fly using only one feather. Essentially, the longer, the better for the fly tyer. A long hackle is great, but if the shaft is too thick or stiff to easily bend around the hook shank, it's not going to be of much use to us. I have a neck or two whose hackles are really nice except that the stems are too stiff and tend to split as you wrap them; the hackles from those necks aren't very useful. What we really want is a hackle with a long, soft shaft.

Barbs. The barbs are the working part of the fly. In a dry fly, they provide the support to float our fly, and, in a wet fly, they are the moving, life-simulating part of the fly. First of all, we would like to have a large number of barbs on our hackle feather. The larger the number of barbs present for each unit of hackle length, the fewer turns or wraps of hackle it will take to develop a broad supporting base for our dry flies, or a greater number of fibres on our wet flies. Secondly, and maybe more importantly, we want the barbs to be really stiff to support a dry fly or really soft to provide the illusion of movement on our wet patterns. In addition to the relative stiffness of the hackle, whether the hackle is suitable for dry-fly or wet-fly use depends on the amount of web present. Web is really the presence of barbules on the feather.

Barbules. If there are a large number of barbules on a feather, we say that it is "webby." Barbules hold the individual barbs together so that they are difficult to separate into individual fibres when the hackle is wound. Also, the fact that the barbules are very close together causes them to absorb water readily through capillary action. This is compounded by the fact that it is difficult to get the fibres to release the water they hold—hard to dry the fly once it is wet. Well then, if we are looking for a hackle to float our fly, we want one with as little web (as few barbules) as possible. On the other hand, for use on wet flies, we want lots of web so that it will absorb water and sink better. Additionally, the stiffness of the barbs is directly related to the amount of web present. The less web, the stiffer the hackle, which delineates further the need for as web-free hackle as we can get for our dry-fly patterns.

One of the old standard methods of checking a neck for dry-fly quality is to flex the neck so that the hackles stand up and then to bend the individual hackles to see if they spring back to their original shape. For some reason, there seems to be a correlation between the stiffness of the hackle stem (which is the only thing you are checking in this case) and the stiffness of the barbs on the hackle. Keep in mind, however, that too stiff a shaft, although perhaps indicating stiff barbs, may actually detract from the tying ability of the hackle. This test really doesn't tell you much, does it?

Besides, on about one of five necks that you test in this manner, the skin will break when you flex it, and then you've bought the neck whether you want it or not. Most importantly, you do not, repeat *not,* have to have a stiff shaft to have stiff barbs. Both the Metz and the Hoffman necks shown in the color photo insert have superbly stiff barbs and very fine, soft shafts. Of course, that's one of the features that they breed for when developing their strains of roosters.

By the way, one of the sure signs of the tyro fly tyer is the individual who picks up a neck, flares a hackle, and then tests it for stiffness by feeling the fibres with his lip. The idea is that the lip, being very sensitive, can better feel if the barbs are stiff. The fallacy, though, is that if the hackle barbs are stiff enough to be worth using on a dry fly, you can feel their stiffness with a calf roper's calloused hands.

Just how, then, should you go about identifying a neck that has really good dry-fly hackle? First of all, by its sheen. In order for a neck to appear shiny, there can't be much web in it. Remember, the web is actually the barbules on the hackle, and they are soft; soft fibres don't reflect much light, just as soft wool fabric isn't shiny. If a neck shines, it's worth looking closer at.

Flex a feather. Just how stiff is the shaft? What you are looking for here is not that it bounces like a spring, which would indicate that the shaft may be too stiff to tie well. It should have some life, though.

Take a quick check on how many barbs the feather has. Remember, the more barbs, the fewer turns or wraps will be needed to adequately hackle the fly. I have a beautiful light ginger neck that only lacks this quality. The color is exceptional, the barbs are nice and stiff, the shaft is fine enough so that the hackles wrap easily, and the feathers are very long for their width. The one bad fault is that there just aren't very many barbs on a hackle. Even though the hackles are long, they still tie a sparse fly.

Last, but probably most important, check the width of the hackle versus its length. Make sure that you flare the hackle to do this! We've all been caught on this one; you find a neck with very long, slim hackles and run to the cash register with it. Arriving home, you find, to your dismay, that those long hackles are only slim because the barbs all lie very close to the stem. You have some nice long hackles with some very long barbs when they are flared. Flare the hackle and if the hackle is five or six times as long as the barbs on one side of the feather, it will tie a good fly. I have a few neck hackle samples that Henry Hoffman sent me, one of which is nearly 13 times as long as the barb length ($\frac{5}{32}''$ barb length on a two-inch hackle); that's a helluva hackle.

If you are looking for a wet-fly hackle, all of the above apply except that you want all of the web that you can get. The web means that the feather is soft and will move easily. Also it will readily absorb water. Don't expect too much in the way of hackle shape. I've never seen a good wet-fly hackle that was really long for its width. It really isn't that important, though, because you usually only take a few turns of hackle on the wet patterns anyway. For really good hackle to use on wets, nymphs, and streamers, hen necks are the answer. We'll talk more about that later.

There is one surefire way to get superb dry-fly hackle and that is to buy hackle from the outfits that raise it commercially just for the fly tyer. We call these the "Feather Factories."

THE FEATHER FACTORIES

In our discussion of hackle so far, mention has been made several times of the commercially raised hackle that is now available to the fly tyer. The Metz Hatchery produces a full line of necks including blue dun, grizzly, black, brown, cream, splashed, cree, and variants in natural colors, and they also offer a bleached ginger. All these colors are also available in hen sets (absolutely the greatest for wet flies) and saddles. Dun, grizzly, and brown account for about 85% of their production and all of the others can be obtained only on an "as available" basis.

Hoffman's Hackle Farm has restricted their production almost entirely to grizzly hackle. Their light grizzly has proven to be very popular, and many tyers, as well as some retailers, use them exclusively by dyeing them to the desired colors. This method allows the tyer to get any color he or she wants while still being able to have the natural barring of the grizzly hackle. They do produce a few white capes and a few creams but they are pretty hard to find as the few that are available are sold quickly.

Just what are the advantages of commercially raised hackle over the imported hackle that most of us usually buy, and how does the actual cost of the two compare?

There are many advantages to the use of commercially raised hackle, the most important of which is quality. Both Metz and Hoffman have spent years developing strains of birds that produce superb dry-fly hackle: long slim feathers; fine, soft stems; hard, stiff barbs; and a minimum of web. For obvious economic reasons, they have developed these strains of superior birds in the rarer colors. Hoffman started his search for the perfect grizzly; while Metz chose the dun colors as his goal.

In the process of developing their strains of roosters, each of them have also had to breed among the more common colors to arrive at the quality they were looking for in their grizzlies and duns. I speculate that in order to get his beautiful light grizzlies, Hoffman either had to get a really good white strain to breed from or, in the process of breeding lighter and lighter, he got a few good whites. However it came about, we now have really good white dry-fly hackle available for the first time. Understand, I'm only speculating; neither of them are giving out a lot of information about the specific processes used in the development of their strains of birds. Nevertheless, from their development of duns and grizzlies, we have ended up with superb quality dry-fly hackle in most colors.

Now, if you are going to raise roosters, you must have some hens to lay the eggs—*voila*, we now have hen hackle available in the rare colors too! It's mighty hard to raise just the front end of a rooster to get neck hackle, the rear just kind of comes along in the bargain, so we end up with saddle hackles as part of the deal. In short, the raisers of commercial hackle for the fly tyer can provide us with quality wet-fly hackle and saddles as well as great dry-fly hackle. The fly tyer can only come out best in such a situation. But what about the cost difference between this "ultimate" hackle and the imported stuff that we've been using for years?

There is no denying that there is a cost difference! A prime imported brown neck at this time is less than one fifth the cost of a Metz brown. This appears to be a great difference, but let's take a look at what we are really getting in each case.

First of all, there is no way that you will get an imported brown neck that even approaches the quality of the Metz—at any price. Ah, now the rationale goes, "The imported brown neck is good enough quality for my flies, the Metz hackle is better than it needs to be, so I'm paying for quality in excess of my needs." That's a good point but if you could have the extra quality for the same money, would you take it? Let's just leave the subject there for now.

That imported brown neck is going to provide you with about 200 usable hackles in the size range from #10 to #16 hackles. Despite what you may have heard about there being four or five hundred usable hackles on a neck, you will find that unless you tie everything clear, up to about 2/0 flies, you aren't going to get nearly that many. All fly tyers have enough necks with all of the hackles from #10 and smaller gone to stuff a feather tick. That Metz neck is going to give you about 400 hackles in the size range from #10 to #20, and you still haven't even touched the #22 to #28 hackles (you didn't even have any on the imported neck). Hackle count isn't the whole story either.

Tying from that imported neck, you are going to need to use at least two hackles per fly because they aren't long enough to hackle a fly adequately. The Metz will tie one fly per hackle. So, our imported neck with 200 hackles will tie 100 flies from #10 to #16s; the Metz will furnish enough hackles to tie 400 flies from #10s to #20s and about another 100 or so in the really small sizes. That's 500 flies! In short, you would need to buy five imported necks to tie the same number of flies as you can get out of the Metz neck, all would be of lesser quality, and none below size 16. If you never use smaller flies you still might opt for the imported brown and save a few bucks, but where are you going to find an imported dun that cheap, or a good light ginger, for that matter?

The same thing applies to the Hoffman "Super Grizzlies." A Hoffman will cost about double what the average, good-quality grizzly will set you back. The Hoffman will tie at least twice as many flies, is better quality hackle, and will tie all the way down to #28s. Your cost per fly is about the same in either case, and that makes the Hoffman a bargain.

If you will check around, you will find that many commercial tyers are now using commercially raised hackle. The guy or gal who is tying for money doesn't spend even an extra penny or two per fly if it can be avoided. When the pros are on to something, it is worth looking into. Part of the reason that the professional tyers use the "fancy" stuff is that, to them, time is money, and if they only need to tie-in and wrap one hackle instead of two, they can finish the fly a little faster. When you start multiplying that "little faster" by dozens, and those dozens by dozens, the commercial tyer is making extra money.

The other reason that commercially raised hackle is the feather of the future is the availability (or lack of it) of decent imported hackle. Those of us who have been tying for any length of time can attest to the difficulty of getting good hackle. Every year the demand grows and every year the number of necks available decreases slightly, hence, the price goes up and the quality goes down. To put it simply, we're running out of good-quality imported hackle.

All right then, maybe the domestic stuff isn't such a bad deal, but why in the world do they have to charge such exorbitant prices? It doesn't cost fifty bucks to raise a chicken! But the guy selling the neck has to make a fair profit so the grower isn't getting fifty dollars. They haven't learned to breed only for roosters either, so there's some time and space lost at that point in the operation. And, you can't tell if the rooster is going to produce really good hackle until he's old enough to kill, so you've had to feed him for a year whether he turns out to be really special or just an also ran.

The grower of frying chickens can take a building with a capacity of 1,000 birds, buy sexed chicks, and have them on the market in nine weeks, weighing five pounds or more. He can empty and fill that building four or five times a year. The grower of hackles has that same building tied up for a full year to raise ⅕ as many birds. In addition, he is feeding full-grown chickens for nearly the full year.

Birds being raised for hackle also have to be caged separately so that they don't fight and destroy one another's reason for being. Because of the value of the product, each bird must have its own separate source of food and water so that one sick bird doesn't wipe out the whole year's work. And, then, of course, there's the "little" things like special feeds that promote feather growth, checking on the roosters so that they are killed at their absolute prime, vaccinating all of them, not to mention the arduous task of killing, skinning, and preparing 50,000 capes and saddles a year.

It seems to me that we are not only getting a great bargain, but that we fly tyers owe a debt of gratitude to these people who have assured the future availability of good-quality hackle for our sons and grandsons. They may never know of jungle cock, but they will know about grizzlies and blue duns.

What does the future hold for commercially raised hackle? Well, first of all, the hackle will keep getting better and better as the breeders have more and more good breeding stock to select from. Secondly, there will surely be others who achieve the quality that Metz and Hoffman have attained. There are already several breeders that are commercially raising hackle and, although their average quality isn't quite up to par with the established raisers, it is very good and will improve as their breeding stock enlarges.

What excites us, though, is the coming of really superb saddle hackle. Henry Hoffman has some that will truly tie #18s and 20s. Not only will they tie that small, you can tie four or five flies (see illustration) out of each hackle! Henry estimates that it will be another couple of years before saddles of this size will be common—but they are coming. He is already producing saddles in the #14-to-#16 range in quantity. Now, when you start getting four or five flies per hackle as opposed to using two hackles per fly, and in the really small sizes, that should excite any fly tyer.

Hoffman saddle hackle

41

three
Synthetic Materials

We are going to make the assumption (always dangerous!) that you already have a basic understanding of the common, natural materials that the fly tyer uses and devote our discussion of materials to the synthetics. This has been, perhaps, the most exciting area in fly-tying for the past several years as new materials, and new uses for long available materials, have rapidly been developed by innovative fly tyers. These materials have resulted in patterns and pattern types that are more realistic, more fishable, and easier tied than many which use traditional materials. We certainly don't advocate the abandonment of natural materials and traditional tying techniques but do feel that the new materials deserve to be included in the repertoire of all advanced fly tyers.

Synthetic materials have been used to some degree, I'm sure, since the second or third fly was tied. My library of old tying books lists such things as Cellophane, rubber products, and Duco cement being used in some patterns. Because the tyers of years ago had a much wider range of natural materials available and, of course, a much smaller selection of synthetics to choose from, the extensive use of synthetic materials is relatively new in the world of fly-tying and there are many techniques that have been developed to handle these materials. In this chapter we will discuss the materials and then cover the applicable techniques in the tying chapters to follow.

Dubbing materials made from synthetics seemed to really get the movement towards artificial materials started. Fly-Rite was the outfit that first got to the market with a good synthetic dubbing material and Dave McCann, of Fly-Rite, was kind enough to provide us with the technical information about the materials and methods used in producing these materials. The following points are what he considers the most important aspects of the materials as they apply to the fly tyer.

Polymer. Without being overly technical, this simply means the type of material. The materials used are polypropylene, nylon, cellulosics, and polyesters. Just about everyone has heard the little tidbit of information that polypropylene has a density of less than 1 and, therefore, floats on water. Dave is adamant in pointing out that it really isn't any big deal. Polypropylene's density is about 0.9 gm/cc which is not enough differential for the dubbing to keep a hook afloat by itself. The floatant that you apply to the fly give it hydrophobic properties that hold the fly up.

Nylon, with a density of about 1.1 gm/cc is very close behind polypropylene. The cellulosics (around 1.3 gm/cc) and the polyesters (1.3 to 1.4 gm/cc) are also well within the range of usable materials. To quote Dave, "Please note that I am not saying that density is an overriding factor in choosing a material—it isn't—but rather just one property to bear in mind."

Diameter. This is really pretty simple, to have the properties of a good dubbing material, the material used must be of the finest diameter possible. The four materials mentioned as being used for synthetic dubbing all can be extruded fine enough to handle easily.

Length. Fibre length is determined by the manufacturer and they all seem to have arrived at about the same standards. There is an advantage to the longer fibres found in synthetic materials, when compared to most furs: The longer fibres make the process of spinning the material onto the thread easier, and the longer fibres are each wrapped around the hook more times as the dubbing is wrapped so that a more durable body is formed. Fly-Rite® is made with a fibre length of about 1½" which seems to be about the average for all brands.

Color. This is an interesting area and one that I had no idea was so involved. The tans and greys are the most difficult colors to get dyed uniformly and Dave says that they throw away about ⅓ of their batches dyed to these shades. Murphy's Law at work again: The tans and greys are, of course, the most used colors.

They have investigated everything that they can think of that might be contributory to the dyeing problem. Well water, fluoridated water, solvents, salt water, temperature, time, types of dyes, and even the materials of which their dye vats are made, have all been checked out and the only conclusion that they have come to is that, "dyeing is still as much of an art as a science, and so we just throw the whole batch out if it's not a good match to the standard."

As with many (if not most) of the items that we use, we tend to take the synthetic dubbing materials for granted, not realizing the effort that that inexpensive little package represents. There are presently three major suppliers of these dubbing materials: Fly-Rite, Creative Anglers, and Andra Spectrum.

Fly-Rite. The folks at Fly-Rite offer their dubbing material in two different formats. First, there is Fly-Rite Extra Fine Poly Dubbing Material which is a polypropylene material in loose form. The average fibre length is about 1½". This is packaged in small zip-lock packages.

Secondly, they offer Poly-II which is nylon polypropylene in sheet form. The fibres are gently pulled from the sheet for dubbing and, if done carefully, the fibres will be about 3" long.

The Fly-Rite® is available in forty colors. Twenty of these are basic colors: black, light tan, cream, golden yellow, and the like. The other twenty colors are blended colors for insect and pattern representation such as Cahill tan, olive sulphur, and Adams grey. The material is available in individual packets or as a portfolio of all forty colors in a clear plastic binder with a pocket for each color. This portfolio is really handy as it means that the tyer has the entire selection readily at hand.

The Poly II comes in 12 basic colors, 8 supplementary colors, and 4 fluorescent colors. The basic colors are the most commonly used colors for fly-tying such as Cahill cream, pale yellow, rust, and cream. The supplementary colors include pale watery olive, dark grey, and pale watery silver. Fluorescent colors are red, orange, yellow, and green. Each sheet is packaged in a small, reclosable bag like that of Fly-Rite®, but because it is in sheet form, you can carry the full selection in even a small, streamside tying kit. Poly II can also be used as a winging material by cutting wings from the sheets or, easier yet, by using a wing former and burning a piece to shape. White, Cahill cream, pale watery silver, and pale watery rose are the most popular for wings. We'll talk more about this in the section on winging materials.

Andra Spectrum. Spectrum is a very soft, easy-to-handle, synthetic dubbing material. It is available in 50 different colors including both basic colors such as black, brown, and pink, and mixed colors such as pale dun-olive, light caddis green, and tan-claret. It is packaged in the same type of reclosable bags as Fly-Rite® and is available as a selection of all 50 colors.

C. A. Ultra Translucent Nymph Dubbing. The Creative Anglers dubbing material is meant primarily for nymphal imitations. It really is translucent and has more of a sparkle to it than either Andra Spectrum or Fly-Rite®. C. A. is available in 40 colors including both basic colors and blended colors such as light yellow stone, light hare's ear, and leech brown. It, too, comes in individual reclosable bags and is available in a binder similar to that of Fly-Rite® containing all 40 colors.

There is one other dubbing material that we should tell you about, but it isn't really a synthetic. It is, however, an innovative product. L & L Products makes a dubbing material, called K-DUB for dry flies that is made from kapok. Kapok, which is a silky fibre from around the seeds of the Malayan ceiba tree, is very buoyant. It was used for many years as the primary filler in life jackets and didn't go unnoticed among fly tyers. It was, however, a difficult material to use as it didn't dub very well and dyeing it always resulted in a muddy looking color. Another problem was that the material matted very easily and so it was difficult to get it smoothly dubbed onto the tying thread. Because of these problems, it never was really accepted as a common material and, although I can find reference to kapok as a tying material in most of the old tying books, I can't find a pattern listed that calls for the material.

L & L found some way to process the kapok so that most of the matting tendency is eliminated, and it dyes to a clear color. After processing and dyeing, the material is then treated with a permanent floatant. Now, don't get too excited; like the polypro, with its density of less than one, the buoyant quality of K-DUB isn't sufficient in itself to support the fly, but does contribute significantly to the floating qualities of the completed imitation. The fibre length of K-DUB is around ½ to ¾ inches, which is somewhat shorter than the synthetic materials but longer than many natural furs and quite usable. It, too, is packaged in small reclosable bags.

The new dubbing materials probably won't ever replace natural fur completely. Natural fur does have a lifelike quality about it that the synthetics lack and, for some types of flies, the fact that you can dub, using the long-guard hairs and the soft underfur at the same time, makes it the material of choice. We are convinced, though, that the synthetics *do* add to the floating ability of our dry flies, and, in particular, the flies dry much faster by false casting. Some of our favorite dry-fly fishing is in the fast pocket of water of our Western streams and you must have a fly that will float well and dry quickly between presentations. The synthetics are much superior to natural furs in meeting our needs in this specialized type of angling.

Dubbing isn't the only body material that has been added to the arsenal of synthetics for the fly tyer. Several years ago, I discovered a material called Cobra® monofilament, put out by Cortland. Cobra® is a flat monofilament line material and I found that it worked beautifully for segmented bodies on larger caddis larva and stonefly and mayfly nymphal imitations. I really felt that I was innovative until one of the store customers looked at what I was doing and commented: "Oh, that's one of Bob Saile's new patterns, isn't it?"

I've learned since then that none of us has the corner on good ideas and it's rather immodest to assume that you are the only one who is capable of "discovering" that great new pattern or material! Along the same line, I "discovered" a method for tying wings on a dry-fly caddis imitation that was dynamite! I took a mallard feather and reversed the fibres, which created a beautiful tent-shaped wing, and the resultant veining was really imitative. We sold several dozen in the store and then quit tying them when it was discovered that the wing was too fragile to be usable.

A couple of years later, the owner of another fly shop in the state had an article published in one of the magazines, showing how to tie *my* fly. I was incensed! It was an obvious case of piracy!

Not too long after that, we purchased some materials from a retired commercial tyer and Bill Blade's *Fishing Flies and Fly Tying* was among the books that came with the deal. Imagine my chagrin when, leafing through the book (published in 1951), I saw the same technique being used. I had made my "discovery" some 25 years or so after Blade's. So, when you hear the talk that so-and-so stole the new pattern from so-and-so, you might stop and consider that maybe each of them arrived at the same (usually pretty obvious) discovery independently. Frank Johnson's uncovering of the material, Swannundaze® is one of real importance to the modern fly tyer and it *was* a discovery—quite literally!

Frank is a truck driver by trade, and he found the material in the backroom of a warehouse. It was used as a decorative trim material, and what they had was the wrong size and in the wrong colors for fly-tying. He saw, however, the potential for its use, contacted the manufacturer, and had him recut a die for the right sizes and produce it in colors suitable for use at the tying bench.

Swannundaze® is a soft plastic material that is slightly half-oval in cross section. That is, one side is flat and the other is rounded. It lends itself naturally for imitation of segmented bodies, much better than the flat monofilament which we talked about earlier.

The material is available in three widths: 1/32″, 1/16″, and 3/32″. The 1/16″ is the most popular size and it is available in 25 colors, including 9 transparent shades, and clear. These transparent colors are most realistic and the clear can be tinted as desired using permanent marking pens.

The Extra Narrow (1/32″) comes in 10 colors, all transparent, and is fine enough to use on small larval and nymphal imitations.

The Wide (³⁄₃₂″) is for large stonefly imitations, primarily, and is made in four transparent colors: clear, dark amber, brown, and black.

By the way, if you wondered about the name of the material, it isn't Swahili for "narrow, oval, plastic"; it's an anagram for Frank's daughters' names, Suzanne and Dawn.

Swannundaze® is packaged in. . ., you guessed it, little reclosable plastic bags. Each bag contains about three yards, which will tie a lot of flies.

Although not really a body material, Peter Phelps, of Phelps Flies, has an interesting and usable product to help in getting the right body shape for stonefly and mayfly nymphs. Many of the nymphs of the aquatic insects have a flattened abdominal section, and these devices are meant to assist in achieving that shape. They are called Nymphorms® and come in three sizes to cover the range for #2 to #12 hooks.

Nymphorms® are die-cut into strips of a plastic material in such a manner that the pieces are left attached to the plastic strip, making them easy to handle. They are cut with six forms per strip and there are six strips per package—good old reclosable bags. The three sizes are color coded: black, large; yellow, medium; and white, small. This feature makes selection of the right size easy and, since the Nymphorm® is completely covered on the finished fly, the color has no bearing on the finished product.

If you are among those who like their flies to be really imitative of the insect, Nymphorm® will help to achieve that desired real life appearance.

Braided, tubular, metallic trim is a synthetic material that has been in use for quite a number of years now for tying the bodies on streamers. Because of its braided construction, the material has a built-in scaly appearance and both the silver and gold colors really reflect light.

Originally, the material was only available constructed from metallic tinsel, but, in recent years, it has been fabricated of Mylar® plastic. The use of Mylar® makes the braid much easier to handle as the problems of working with thin metal strips (tinsel) is eliminated. Mylar® doesn't cut your thread, is softer than tinsel, and, probably most important, the Mylar® isn't subject to tarnishing like metal tinsel material.

There are a couple of special techniques used for tying streamers using the material, and we will discuss and illustrate those in the tying chapters.

Mylar® tinsels are also available in most of the sizes and styles that are called for in the more traditional fly patterns. As mentioned, they are much easier to handle than the true metallic tinsels and are also more durable. In fact, the flat tinsels are even available with a gold finish on one side and silver on the other, thereby eliminating the need for two spools of tinsel in each size.

Rubber products (actually most of them are synthetic rubber) have also found their way to the tying bench. Don was using strips cut from a bicycle innertube for the segmented abdomen on stonefly nymph imitations fifteen years ago. Natural latex rubberbands were used to represent the abdomen on the light-colored representations. Although both of these materials can be replaced now by the use of Swannundaze®, they still are valid materials for the tyer.

Dental dam material is another rubber material that has become very popular for use in imitating segmented bodies on flies. It comes in three different thicknesses and in both a light amber color and a dark grey. The material comes in 5″ by 5″ squares which offers the advantage over rubber-bands or Swannundaze® of being large enough to cut wing cases from for nymphal imitations. Another feature of the material is that it can be easily "dyed" using permanent marking pens.

Synthetic yarns are another source of body materials for the fly tyer. Orlon, Herculon®, Mohlon®, and polypropylene yarns can all be used, and in some pretty innovative ways! Gary LaFontaine developed an emerging caddis pupa pattern using "sparkle yarn" (a synthetic yarn, available under several brand names) that actually imitates the light refraction created by the air sack surrounding the insect.

Don was using a rather strange-colored dry fly one day and I asked what he had used for the body dubbing; after swearing me to secrecy, he admitted to "borrowing" a couple of loops from his wife's shag rug. The point here is that simply because the material is produced in yarn form, you aren't obligated to use it in that manner. Some of the shaggiest dubbing material that you can mix is that containing synthetic yarn fibres and it also adds a translucent sheen to the dubbing.

Wing Materials. Probably because the wing is such an obvious part of a dry fly, the fly tyer has diligently tried to develop better winging material and has often turned to man-made materials. One of the common approaches was to print a piece of thin celluloid with lines to represent the veining in an insect's wing and then to cut the wing shape from the sheet. Herter's and Veniard's even made these available in several die-cut sizes, but they never became very popular. The stiff, unyielding wings acted as efficient propellers to spin the leader into knots as the fly was cast unless the wings were mounted absolutely symmetrical. They also added considerable weight to a dry fly, and it was questionable if the gain of better imitation was worth the losses of more weight and leader twist.

We've come back to the approach, though. L & L Products is marketing a material which uses synthetic fibres pressed into a thin sheet. It is called Microweb. Microweb is much lighter than the old celluloid wing material, and since it is much softer, it has less tendency to whirl the fly during casting; although mounting the wings true is still critical. One of the best features of the Microweb wing is that it is very durable. Also, since the material won't absorb water, thereby adding weight to the fly, the wing can't detract from the floating qualities. Microweb is just as usable for wings on adult stonefly, caddis fly, and many terrestrial insect imitations as it is for mayfly wings.

The material comes in ten colors from white through black. Additionally, the white is easily tinted to any desired shade using permanent marking pens. It is an interesting, usable material that is truly versatile.

As briefly mentioned before, Poly II, Fly-Rite's sheet-formed dubbing material can also be used as a winging material by cutting the desired wing shapes from the sheets. Poly II is somewhat softer than Microweb and, in our experience, a little easier to use for really small flies.

Fly-Rite makes two colors of Poly II expressly for use as winging material: pale watery silver, and pale watery rose. Many of their standard colors are also usable, notably white, Cahill cream, medium grey, and pale watery olive.

Not being overly fond of the time and work involved in assembling cut-wing mayfly imitations, we just don't use them very often. For us, the standard winging material has become polypropylene yarn.

Polypro yarn wings are easier to tie than any other type, are practically indestructible, provide a good silhouette (good enough, unless the trout are being *really* selective), and are highly visible to the angler.

Polypro yarn is available in all shades that you might want for winging. It comes in several different sizes but since the yarn isn't twisted, it is easily separated so that you can use the right amount for the size of fly that you're winging. We'll discuss its use, in detail, in the tying section.

There are also two synthetic products that are meant as artificial hair: Fishair® and Poly Wiggle.

Fishair® is meant as a substitute for long-fibred hairs such as bucktail, calftail, and, in particular, polar bear. It is furnished in four different hair lengths (2-½″, 4″, 6″, and 10″), and in 20 different colors.

The "hair" is set into a stiff backing that is easily broken into smaller pieces for easier handling and storing. It does lack some of the sheen of the natural materials and won't entirely replace the common natural hairs. It is an important addition for those patterns that call for polar bear (very difficult to find, finally protected as it should be), and for use on larger streamers, steelhead, and saltwater flies that require really long-hair fibres.

Poly Wiggle, from Fly-Rite, is polypropylene extruded slightly thicker than that used for dubbing, and formed with fibres 6″ long. It has a pronounced "breathing" action in the water (much better than marabou) and is really bright with a sparkling, translucent sheen.

Poly Wiggle is available in 16 different colors. As a material for large streamer and saltwater flies, Poly Wiggle offers the fly tyer an opportunity to really experiment and innovate. Neat stuff!

Tyers have, for years, searched for the perfect material to use as the head cement to finish their flies. Varnish, lacquer, cements, and fingernail polish have all been recommended and used. Enter, synthetic material! The Prices produce a head cement that is absolutely the best thing that has happened to fly-tying in years. Two coats of this on the finished head and it looks as if it were made of porcelain! For really great heads on salmon flies, streamers, and steelhead flies where the head should be finished perfectly smooth, it just has no equal. It comes in a bottle with a small brush attached to the cap so that it is quick to apply to the fly. It does tend to thicken rather quickly in the bottle so make sure that you get some thinner when you buy the cement.

There is no question that the use of synthetic material is a permanent part of the fly-tying scene as the natural materials become more and more difficult to obtain. The modern tyer needs to keep abreast of the development of these materials and include the techniques for handling them in his list of tying skills. Undoubtedly, some of the innovations will be short-lived and some will be replaced with better ideas but that only serves to keep fly-tying the interesting, enjoyable pursuit that it should be.

Hackle Identification.   1. Silver Badger   2. Badger   3. Cream   4. Light Ginger   5. Ginger   6. Brown   7. Furnace   8. Coachman   9. Blue Dun   10. Brown and Cream   11. Cream Variant   12. Ginger Variant   13. Dark Cree   14. Ginger Particolor   15. Brown Particolor   16. Grizzly   17. Ginger (Fiery Red) Saddle   18. Dun Saddle   19. Grizzly Saddle

Photography by Ritch Phillips

1. Fly-Rite Poly Wiggle   2. Fly-Rite Ultra Fine Poly   3. Fly-Rite Poly II

(left) Commercially raised hackle

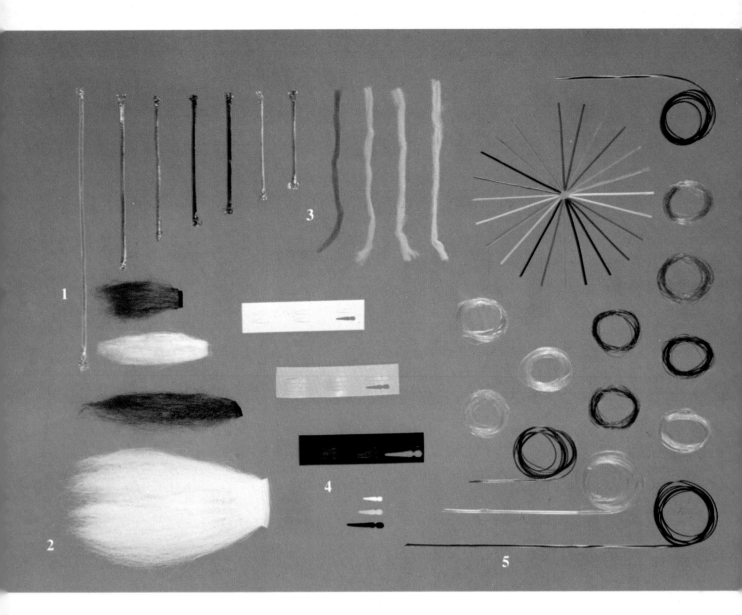

1. Mylar® Tubing   2. Fishair   3. Poly Yarn   4. Nymphorms   5. Swannundaze®

four
Hooks

The only reason for the tying of flies is to entice the fish to accept the angler's offering and, thus, attach itself to the hook. The hook, then, serves a much more important function than merely providing a base for the attachment of the fly-tying materials. In an attempt to better meet the combined requirements of providing a suitable size tying base for proper imitation of the food forms the tyer is trying to imitate, while still maintaining proper hooking qualities, a great number of styles and sizes of hooks have been developed. It is important for the fly tyer to have an understanding of the various styles and sizes so that he can select the proper hook for the use he has in mind. As important as this is, it is also very difficult because each manufacturer has his own method of sizing, styling, and naming of the hooks within his line. There is no standard and that causes some confusion to all of us when trying to work with hooks outside of the line that we normally use.

In order to begin to understand the relationship of one hook to another, it is necessary to know exactly what we are talking about when we refer to a particular part of a hook.

Eye: The eye of the hook is that part to which we attach our leader. *Shank:* The shank is the upper part of the hook, extending from the eye to the bend. *Bend:* The bend is the curved part of the hook which joins the upper and lower sections. *Point:* The point is the section of the hook from the lower part of the bend to the sharp tip. *Barb:* The barb of the hook is the small sharp piece that points back towards the bend. *Gap:* The gap (or gape) is the distance between the tip of the point and the shank. *Throat:* This is the distance from the tip of the point to the back of the bend.

Each of these parts of the hook has an influence on the ability of the hook to do its job of hooking and holding the fish as well as contributing to the appearance and effectiveness of an artificial fly. Let's take a closer look at each part.

Eye. There are three common types of eyes on fly-tying hooks: the tapered eye, the ball eye, and the looped eye. The ball eye is formed by wrapping the end of the shank around a wire rod of the proper size for the hook; the diameter of the wire forming the eye is the same as the diameter of the hook shank.

The tapered eye is formed in the same manner but the end of the shank is tapered before the eye is formed. This results in an eye with the same inside diameter as the ball eye but with a smaller outside diameter due to the tapering of the wire, which gives a small decrease in weight and also provides for less bulk in the head area of the finished fly.

Tapered eye

Ball eye

Looped eye

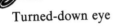

Turned-down eye

Turned-up eye

Ring eye

Round shank

Forged shank

The loop eye is formed by wrapping the shank around a rod as were the ball and tapered eyes, but instead of just bringing the end of the wire to the completion of a circle against the shank, the wire is brought back along the shank for a short distance. This eye design is of advantage for tying streamer, steelhead, and salmon flies where there is a large amount of material attached to the top and bottom of the hook shank at the head of the fly. The added width of the hook provided by the two thicknesses of wire serves to offset the bulk of the materials on the top and bottom of the hook, resulting in a more symmetrical finished head on the fly.

The angle of the eye in relation to the hook shank is also a subject of discussion when speaking of the eye of the hook. The eye may be turned up from the shank (away from the point) which is designated as a *TUE* (turned-up eye). If the eye is turned down from the shank (towards the point), the hook is called a turned-down eye and abbreviated as a *TDE*. A hook with the eye in line with the shank is called a ringed hook, or a ring-eyed hook. Each of these designs offer some advantages and disadvantages so we'll discuss each one in detail.

The turned up eye (TUE) is most often used for small-sized dry flies where the short shank, combined with a small gap, would leave very little room between a turned-down eye and the hook point, decreasing the chances of successfully hooking a fish. The turned-up eye clears the eye away from the hooking area. The main disadvantage to the turned-up eye is that the motion created in setting the hook tends to cause the point to rotate back and away from the fish.

The turned-down eye (TDE) has the advantage of rotating the point towards the fish as the hook is set, resulting in more efficient hooking of the fish. The disadvantage of the turned-down eye is that the eye is tipped down into the hooking area of the hook effectively decreasing the size of the gap. As mentioned before, this is only a problem when tying on very small hooks. The turned-down eye hooks are the type most commonly used by the fly tyer.

The ring-eyed hooks are a compromise for dry-fly use: the eye in line with the shank provides no rotational hooking advantage as found with a turned-down eye, but doesn't close off any of the gap either. In short, it doesn't have the disadvantage of rotating the hook away from the fish as the hook is set, the way the turned-up eye does, but doesn't offer the advantage of rotating the point into the fish either. The most often-claimed advantage of the ring-eyed hooks is that they provide for freer movement of streamers and other underwater flies. The ring eye may well be the best compromise but, unfortunately, there are very few styles of fly-tying hooks available with this type of eye.

Shank. The shank of the hook is where the fly tyer plies his skill; this is where all of the tying materials are attached. Other than length and diameter (which we will discuss when looking at hook sizing), the shank of the hook is very simple. The shank is either round, in which case it is left in the form of the wire used for the hook construction, or the shank is nearly rectangular, which is called a forged shank. The reason for forging is to restructure the wire (particularly in the area of the bend) so that the wire is thicker and, hence, stronger in the direction that force is applied. This enables the hookmaker to provide us with a lighter hook, because he can use finer wire, which still has sufficient strength. This is of particular importance in dry-fly hooks where minimum weight is desirable.

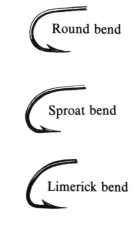

Round bend

Sproat bend

Limerick bend

Bend. The bend is considered the part of the hook from where the shank ceases to be straight to the back of the barb. There are a myriad of different shapes to this curved area and each manufacturer has his own ideas as to what the bend area of the hook should be like for the most effectiveness. Fly-tying hooks are mostly found with either a round bend, a sproat bend, or a limerick bend.

A round bend means simply that shape of the hook in the area of the bend is a portion of a circle. This is the most common bend shape for tying hooks, particularly for those meant for use for dry flies. One claimed advantage of the round bend is that once the fish is hooked, the tendency is for the fish to exert its force well up in the bend area, more in line with the shank and the fisherman's leader. This also is the area of the bend with the greatest strength.

A sproat bend is in the form of a slightly parabolic curve. Typically, a sproat-bend hook has a shorter point than a round bend, which possibly makes for easier hooking of the fish. Because the sharpest part of the curve is at the bottom of the curve, just behind the point, the weight of the fighting fish is in that area. Some feel that this offers the fish a better chance of "throwing" the hook. What may be of importance to the fly tyer is the fact that a sproat bend starts further towards the eye of the hook than a round bend and, thus, shortens the straight length of the shank, when a round bend and a sproat bend of the same size are compared. Where the tyer would like to have a slightly down-angled tail, as on some nymphs, the sproat bend lends itself quite well.

Limerick-bend hooks have a bend with a more exaggerated parabolic curve. This results in an even greater shortening of the shank as the bend is blended into the shank even farther towards the eye than on a sproat bend hook. The limerick bend ends at the point with a very sharp curve so that the weight of the fish is carried very low on the hook, immediately behind the barb. Most limerick hooks that are used for fly-tying are salmon hooks. As with the sproat bend, the limerick shape may be of some advantage where the tyer would like to have a down-angled tail to give some curve shape to the insect being represented, such as a freshwater shrimp pattern.

Point. The term "point" may mean as many as three different things when used in reference to hooks. The area from the end of the bend (the point at which the barb was cut from the shank) to the sharp tip of the hook is called the point. The sharp tip of the hook, itself, is also called the point. There is also a "point" at the very rear of the barb. Let's talk, first of all, about the point in its broadest sense—the portion from the end of the bend to the tip of the hook.

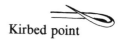

Kirbed point

Straight point

Reversed point

The entire point section of the hook may either be in line with the shank of the hook, offset to the left as one looks at the shank from the front, or offset to the right when seen from the front.

A straight hook has the point in line with the shank and is by far the most common type of point used for fly-tying. Supposedly the reason for this is

51

that it makes it easier for the hook to balance evenly when used for dry flies and to move in a straighter manner when used for wet flies, nymphs, and streamers.

A hook with the point offset to the right of the shank (when observed from the front, with point down) is said to be "kirbed." A hook which has the point offset to the left is referred to as a "reversed" hook. There is some advantage to having the point of the hook turned out from in line with the shank. On very small hooks where the gap is very narrow, the actual hooking of the fish can be difficult. An offset point is moved out from under the shank resulting in a much increased gap.

This past fall, we were fishing on the South Platte and the fish weren't interested in anything larger than #22 dry flies. I noticed quickly that although I was getting plenty of takes to my fly, Don was the only one hooking any fish. I went down to where he was, watched for a while, and when I wasn't able to detect anything he was doing differently, I asked him about it. He had gently offset the point a little on his fly. I followed suit and immediately started hooking some fish.

I really can't see where it matters whether the point is offset to the right or left, but on small hooks I am convinced that the offset point results in more efficient hooking of the fish.

Another subject that falls under the heading of points is the actual sharp tip off the hook. The sharp point of the hook may be shaped in several different ways: Spear point, hollow-ground, and round are the most common types found on tying hooks.

Round point

A spear point will have a straight line from the tip of the hook to the tip of the barb, but there will be a slight curve ground on the bottom side of the point.

A hollow point will be essentially the opposite of the spear point, that is the bottom line of the hook will be straight from the tip of the hook to the bend, but there will be a concave curve from the tip of the hook to the point of the barb. This results in a finer, more tapered point than the spear point. Since the shaping of the hollow-ground point entails a more difficult operation than that used for the spear point, these hooks will cost a little more.

Hollow point

Spear point

Both the spear point and the hollow-ground point are shaped with the sides of the point flat; this is where they differ from the round point. On a round point, the hook is sharpened so that the round shape of the wire is maintained: the same shape as a sharpened pencil. Which point shape is the most efficient is debatable; much more relevant is the shape of the barb.

As the barb of the hook becomes lower and shorter, the easier the point can penetrate past the barb and the less force is needed to set the hook. This is where the advantage of the hollow-ground point shows up: It has a lower barb for more of the distance from the point of the hook to the point of the barb. A round-point hook may or may not have the advantage of the lower barb depending on how the maker shapes the hook. The ultimate ease of penetrating the hook is found on those hooks that have no barb at all.

Barbless hooks have become increasingly popular in the United States during the last few years due to the increased awareness of the advantages of releasing our fish unharmed. The purpose of a barb on a hook point is to keep the fish from being able to disengage the hook back out through the hole formed when the hook penetrated. Those of us who have fished with barbless hooks question whether the lack of a barb results in an increased number of lost fish. It is difficult to determine any difference.

There is a difference in the number of fish hooked, however. The lack of a barb on the point allows the hook to penetrate the lip of the fish much easier, partly because there is less mass of metal than with a barb present, and partly because a barbless hook is usually sharper when received from the manufacturer (it's easier to sharpen) and is easier to keep sharp on the stream. Flattening the barb on your hooks prior to tying the fly will give you much the same result.

The reason that barbless hooks aren't used much more by fly tyers is that they are only available in a few selected styles and the fact that they are more expensive than barbed hooks. This last point irritated me to no end because, to my way of thinking, not forming a barb was eliminating one step in the hook-making process and, if anything, should mean that the hooks were less expensive to manufacture. After looking into the subject more deeply, I found out why they cost more.

When a hook is made, one of the first steps is to cut the barb into the shank; the wire is still straight at this point. When the time comes to bend the hook into shape, the barb is what is used to hold the tip of the hook as the wire is bent around the mandrel. Without the barb present, the manufacturer has to modify his machinery to hold the point of the wire in another manner (the point of the wire is held between two posts, which is why you will see a small mark on the bottom side of the point on a barbless hook). This added setup and change in the machinery is why we pay more for a hook without a barb than for one with a barb.

That pretty well covers everything you might need to know about the common range of fly-tying hooks other than the methods used for sizing hooks and, of course, the nomenclature used to identify the sizes. Since there is no industry standard, we will save that discussion until we can talk about specific manufacturers. There are a few styles of hooks that we use for fly-tying that are much different from those we have already discussed and we'll just have to take them individually.

Other Hooks. Hooks with more than one shank so that a nymph body shape is established before tying; hooks designed so that they float or ride in the water with the hook point-up instead of down; and hooks with the shank formed nearly in the shape of a circle are all outside of the norm for fly-tying hooks, but tyers have indicated a need for them and the manufacturers have responded.

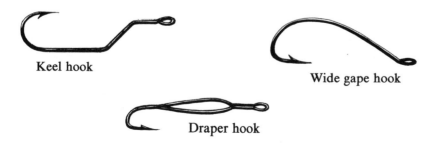

Keel hook

Wide gape hook

Draper hook

The Draper Flat Bodied Hooks are made by Partridge of Redditch, England. These hooks have two shanks which are joined a short distance behind the eye, flare apart, and then taper back to rejoin at the start of the bend. They are used to tie flies imitative of the flat-bodied nymphs, primarily stonefly patterns. Lead can be added between the shanks during the tying process if a weighted version is desired.

Keel hooks are manufactured by Wright & McGill in the United States and are designed so that the point of the hook is up between the wings on the fly. This is of some advantage for streamers and other underwater flies that are to be fished in brushy or weedy waters; the fly is practically impossible to hang up on underwater obstructions. They also make this hook in a fine wire version for dry flies but the advantage for dry flies escapes me.

All of the hook manufacturers already had hooks in their lines called "wide-gape" hooks. These hooks were shaped in the form of a curve all the way from the eye to the point. Some fly tyer's eye was caught by these and he realized their potential for the imitation of caddis larva. They were originally designed as bait hooks but you can now find them in every catalogue dealing with tying materials.

There are quite a few manufacturers of hooks around the world, but there are four major manufacturers who provide hooks to the fly tyers in the United States. Each of these manufacturers has its own sizing method for the hooks in its line, and each uses a different system for identifying its hooks. Since there is no standard among them, we will cover each one separately and then attempt to provide you with a list to show which hooks from which manufacturers are comparable.

O. Mustad & Son (Norway). This is the largest hook manufacturer in the world, at one time advertising 60,000 *different kinds* of hooks. The Mustad company started manufacturing hooks in 1877 after producing a variety of products including steel wire, nails, horseshoe nails, beginning in 1832. Although they probably provide more fly-tying hooks than all of the other makers combined, fly-tying hooks are a very small part of their business. Their latest catalogue shows 47 different styles of fly-tying hooks, ranging in size from 10/0 to #28.

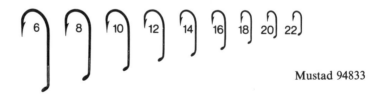

Mustad 94833

Styles: Mustad supplies tying hooks ranging in style from their Quality Number 9523, a 5X short-shank midge hook to Quality Number 3582, double salmon hooks. They make tying hooks with turned-up, turned-down, and ring eyes; round and forged shanks; sproat-bend, limerick-bend, and round-bend. You may choose from hollow-point or spear-point (their term is superior-point). And they do make a few styles of barbless hooks. The accompanying photos will give you a much better idea of their selection than describing them.

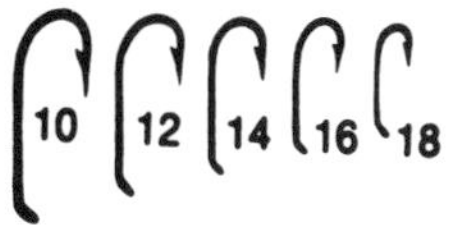

Mustad 94838

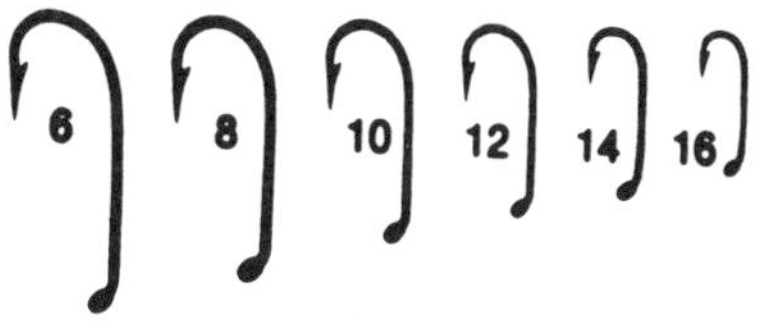

Mustad 94840

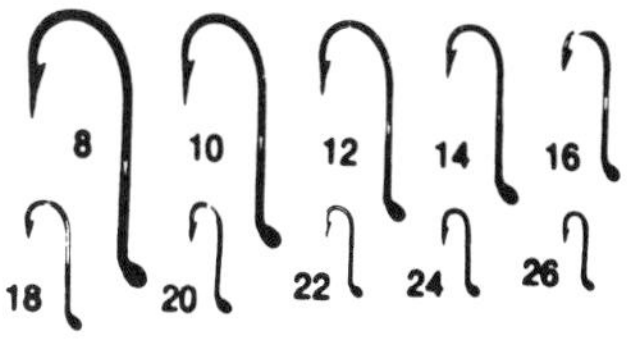

Mustad 94842

Sizes: When we speak of the size of a hook, we are really only speaking of the width of the hook gap. Even this designation will vary somewhat between styles of hooks. To quote from their catalogue, "The size of a fish hook is determined by its pattern; it is given in terms of the width of the gap of the hook." They then show all the sizes of their Mustad-Viking Pattern and continue with: "All hooks of the Mustad-Viking Pattern conform to these sizes." Then comes the clincher, "The hook sizes of other patterns are bound to differ to some extent; the quality number and size should therefore always be quoted together, and regarded as inseparable."

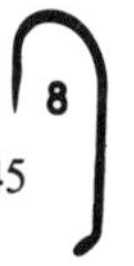

Mustad 94845

(Courtesy Mustad [USA], Inc.)

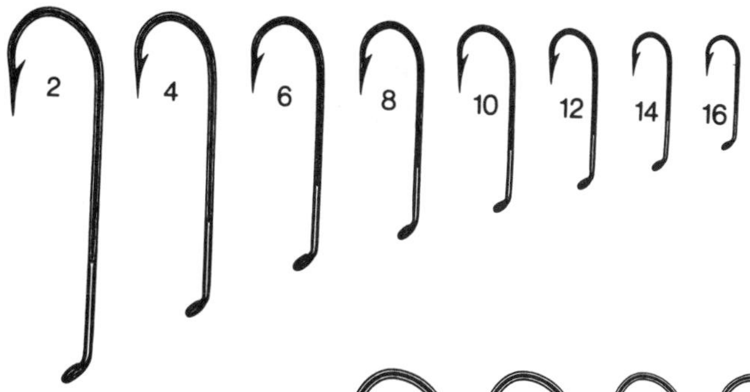

Mustad 9672 (Courtesy Mustad [USA], Inc.)

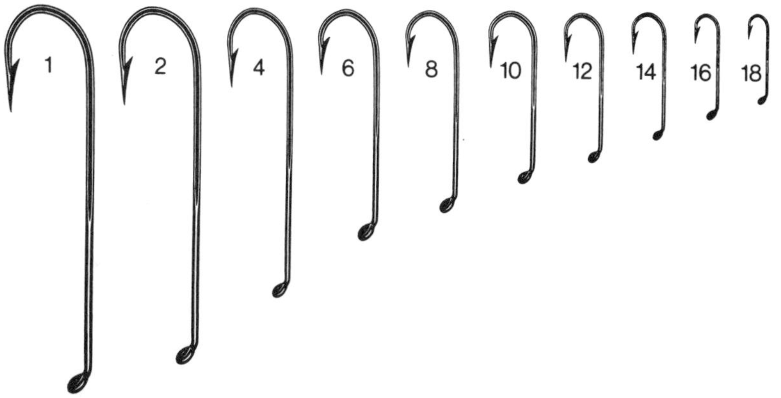

Mustad 79580 (Courtesy Mustad [USA], Inc.)

Essentially the system works in this manner: we begin with a hook size 1, as the hooks get smaller the number-designating size gets larger, e.g. 2, 4, 6, . . . , 28. As hooks get larger from the hook size 1, we start adding oughts (0) to the numbers, ex. 1/0, 2/0, 3/0, . . . , 10/0. Most (not all) fly-tying is done on hooks in the size range from 2 through 28 and Mustad, like most manufacturers, makes hooks only in the even-numbered sizes.

Keep in mind that the hook-size number is only an indication of the width of the gap of the hook; we still must have a means of describing the length of the shank and the relative thickness of the wire.

55

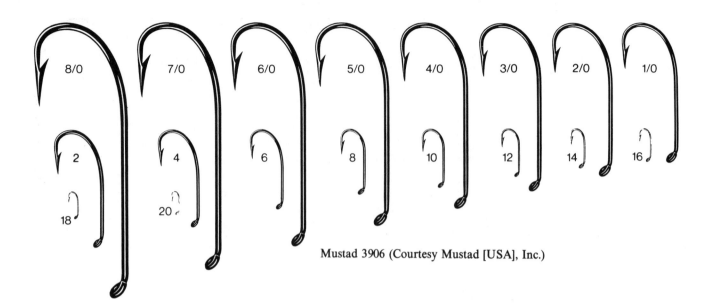

Mustad 3906 (Courtesy Mustad [USA], Inc.)

On a standard hook, the length of the shank is roughly about twice as long as the gap of the hook. Lengths different from this are designated by the uses of Xs. A 1X long hook has a shank length equal to a standard hook one size larger, and although they only supply hooks in even sizes, a #12, 1X long hook will have a hook shank of the same length as a #11 hook. For hooks with a shorter-than-standard shank, the designation is -X short, i.e., a #12, 1X short hook would have a shank the same length as a standard #13 hook.

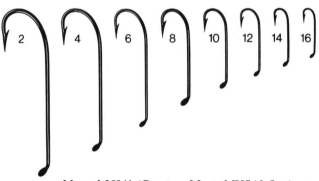

Mustad 38941 (Courtesy Mustad [USA], Inc.)

Relative wire sizes is denoted in much the same way. A hook made from heavier (larger diameter) wire than standard for a given hook size is designated as a "stout," with Xs to indicate how much the wire is oversized. For example, a #12, 2X stout hook would be made with wire normally used for a #10 standard hook. Hooks made with smaller diameter (lighter) wire than normal are called "fine." A #12, 2X fine hook would use wire of the diameter normally used on a #14 hook.

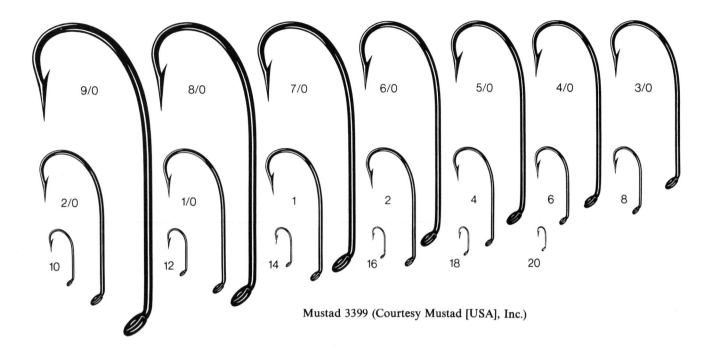

Mustad 3399 (Courtesy Mustad [USA], Inc.)

Wright & McGill (*Eagle Claw*), (*USA*). Eagle Claw is far and away the largest hook manufacturer in the United States. As with Mustad, the vast majority of their hook production is for the bait fisherman, but they do produce fly-tying hooks in 12 basic styles and in the size range from 3/0 to #18.

Styles: Eagle Claw offers hooks for the fly tyer with turned-up eyes, turned-down eyes, and ring eyes. Shank lengths are available from 4X long to 4X short. Bend shapes include round bend and sproat bend. All of their barbed tying hooks appear to be hollow-ground and they offer two styles of barbless hooks, a 1X fine-wire dry-fly hook and a 3X long, standard wire hook for nymphs and streamers. The dry-fly hooks are available from size 4 through size 18, while the streamer/nymph style covers the size range from 1 through 8. Of special note are their keel hooks which were mentioned earlier.

Eagle Claw #59/159

Eagle Claw #60/57

Eagle Claw #61

Sizes: The Eagle Claw line falls a little short in the area of hook-sizing for the fly tyer. Most of their styles are available in sizes from 4 to 18. They do have streamer hooks that cover the larger sizes pretty well (#1 is the largest other than their stainless keel hook which is available in 3/0), but there are many times that the tyer feels the need for flies smaller than #18s. The sizing of their hooks seems to follow pretty closely that used by Mustad, and they do use the same X designations for wire diameter and shank length.

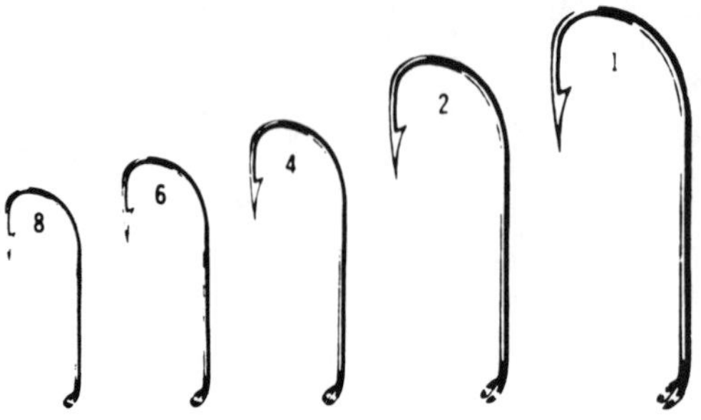

Eagle Claw #1197

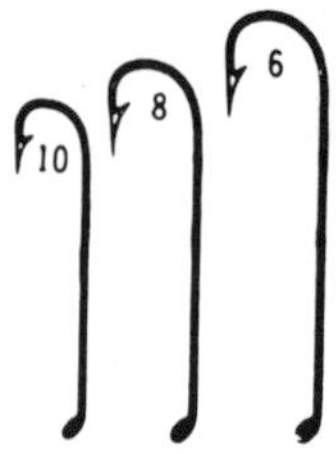

Eagle Claw #281

If we use Mustad as the standard, and that seems best since their hooks are the most commonly used by tyers, the Eagle Claw hooks are a little softer than you are used to. I have used their barbless hooks rather extensively (available through Bob Jacklin of West Yellowstone, if you can't find them) and have never experienced any problem with their fish-holding ability. The dry-fly version is a standard-length hook and if you are used to using the Mustad 94840, you will find the Eagle Claw hooks about 1X shorter. Again, this presents no problem, either in the tying or in properly representing most insects. I get the feeling that this difference in size is a function of the company's sizing standard being slightly different than Mustad's rather than a matter of the Mustad 94840 being a 1X long hook since Mustad doesn't list the 94840 as being 1X long.

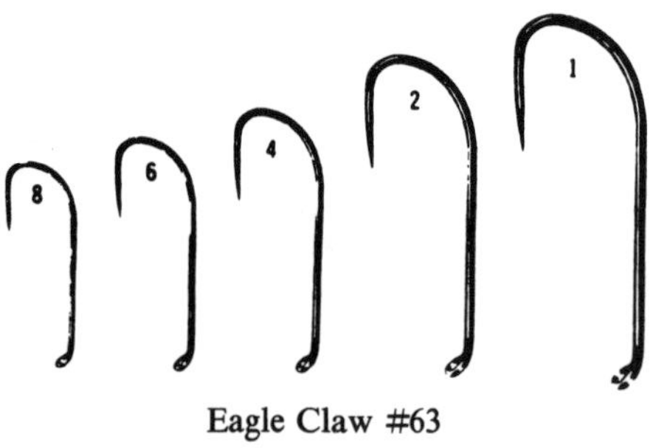

Eagle Claw #63

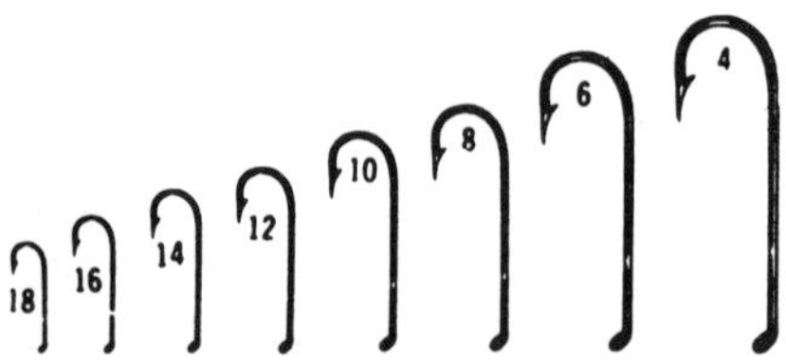

Eagle Claw #64

Eagle Claw hooks have one decided advantage over the others—price! They cost roughly half as much as the imported tying hooks. I sure wish they would expand their line a bit and increase their size range, though.

Eagle Claw keel hooks, #1213

VMC (*France*). The initials VMC stand for Viellard, Migeon et Cie (Viellard, Migeon, and Company). The company was actually started in the 1640s but has been producing fine steel products under the VMC name since 1796 when a Swedish soldier, who had been fighting in France, wed the daughter of Messr. Migeon whose family started the ironworks. In a sense, then, it has been a family operation for about 340 years now. The company began making hooks in 1910, using patterns developed by the famed English fly fisherman, Geoffrey Bucknall. Their operation has been modernized with all new hook-making machines within the past 10 to 12 years and their hooks are now all machine-made using Swedish steel wire.

The VMC hooks are beautifully made with a very low, short barb. All of the hooks are hollow-ground and the samples that we received were all incredibly sharp. The hooks have only been available in the United States for less than two years now but have become quite popular. The company plans on increasing the number of styles and sizes of tying hooks as a sufficient market develops.

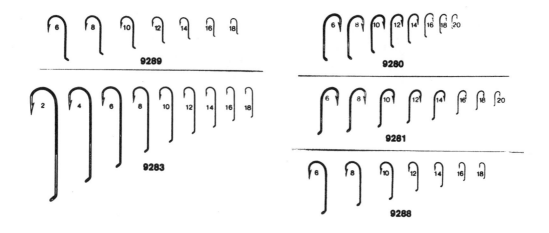

VMC hooks

59

The price of the VMC hooks is slightly higher than either Mustad or Eagle Claw but the hooks are exceptionally well made, nicely tempered, and their point and barb are definitely superior to Mustad or Eagle Claw.

Partridge (England). The area around Redditch, England is generally conceded to be the birthplace of the modern fishing hook, probably due to the fact that there was a monastery located there centuries ago whose monks specialized in the making of quality steel and needles. One hundred years ago, most of the English hook firms were located at Redditch: Allcook, Sealy, Hewitt, Bartlett, Beard, Moore, and Partridge were just some of the names that were associated with quality fish hooks and with the town of Redditch. Of this famous group, only Partridge remains today. Partridge is still a small firm, employing about fifty people and producing "only" about 20 million hooks a year. That sounds like a lot of hooks but compared to Mustad and the other big manufacturers, 20 million hooks may be one day's production. Partridge hooks are still handmade, much in the same way that they were 100 years ago. Each hook is handled, and thus inspected, during nearly each step of production and then given a close final inspection as they are hand-packaged! They may well be the finest hooks that money can buy.

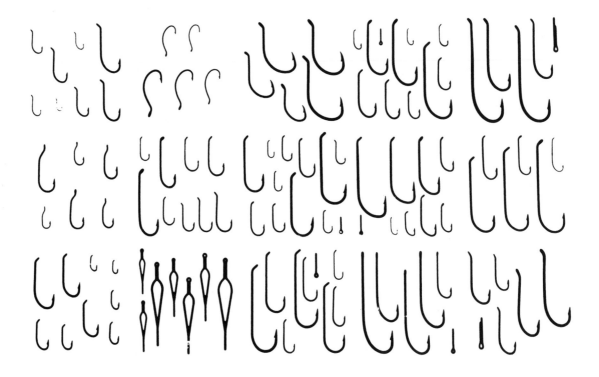

Styles: Partridge produces about fifty standard patterns and an additional twenty or so "special" styles that are made for individuals to their specifications. Because of the fact that most of their operation is still accomplished by hand, even *you* could have them make up a thousand or so of that "perfect" hook that you have been designing for years. Their standard styles include up-eye, down-eye, and the ring-eyed hooks; sproat-bend, round-bend, limerick, and Wilson bends, as well as modifications of each of these. Their hooks all have either a ball eye or a loop eye.

Sizes: Sizes are available from 9/0 salmon hooks to a beautiful #28 midge hook designed by Vince Marinaro. Virtually all styles of Partridge hooks are available in a range from, at least, #8 to #20. They use the same designation for hook length and wire size as was described earlier but their sizing method *is* different.

The hook-sizing method is *not* dependent on the width of the gap of the hook but, rather, on a combination of straight shank length, style of hook, and gap width. Mr. Alan Bramley, Managing Director of Partridge, makes some valid arguments for this approach but also agrees that in order for the tyer to get the hook he wants, he needs to have the Partridge size chart in hand when ordering. In general, however, their sizes are close enough to the more common Mustad sizes, in the more common hook types, so that you can order by size and get essentially what you are expecting.

The Partridge hooks have a very short, very low barb and are the only hooks we know of that are made with a round point. They really are the finest form of the hookmaker's art. Because these hooks are almost entirely handmade, they are considerably more expensive than the other brands we have discussed. Even at that, we are talking about spending less than a dime per fly for the hook.

Fly-tying is a very fast-growing pursuit around the world and as the number of tyers increase the hook manufacturers will be more receptive to our needs and desires. At the present time it seems that the biggest void is in the selection (or lack of it) of barbless hooks. Wouldn't it be great if every manufacturer offered each style of tying hook that they make in a barbless version?

	Standard Dry Fly	TUE Dry Fly	Barbless Dry Fly	2X Long Streamer	3X Long Streamer	Nymph/ Wet Fly
MUSTAD	94840	94842	94845	9671	9672	3906 (B)
	code	code	code	code	code	code
PARTRIDGE	A	B	E3AY	H1A	D4A	L1A
VMC	9288	9289	—	—	9283	9281
EAGLE CLAW	59	—	61	63	58	281

five
Tailing

What do you call it? Which pattern is that? Why doesn't it have a name? These are some of the questions that we commonly get when we tie in public. For some reason, most people seem to think that a fly without a name is incapable of catching fish! The naming of fly patterns supposedly serves several purposes: It provides us with a common reference as to what materials are used and the methods employed in tying a particular imitation, it provides the retailer with a name to use when offering flies for sale, and it allows tyers to communicate with each other more readily.

In reality, though, the naming of patterns really achieves very little for any of us. Order a Muddler Minnow from ten sources and we'll guarantee that you will receive at least seven different patterns and probably none of them will duplicate the original. Order some Light Cahills from a shop in the West and some from a tyer in the Catskills and you'll have two totally different types of flies, although the same materials are used in each. The reason is simple: We each tie for the type of water that *we* fish and, therefore, adapt that original pattern to get better results during our fishing time. That's understandable and as it should be, but it pretty well eliminates the "common reference" reason for naming flies, doesn't it?

The real problem with the naming of patterns is that so many tyers change the color of the wing, the type of tail, the style of wing, the body material, or some other small aspect of the pattern to meet their needs, and then feel obligated to name it and add another pattern to the list.

In Donald DuBois' book, *The Fisherman's Handbook of Trout Flies,* (New York: A. S. Barnes & Co., 1960), he lists 5,939 patterns including over 50 Green Drakes, 33 Pale Evening Duns, and 9 Rio Grande Kings. What it really amounts to is that a pattern name means very little to anyone. The approach that the advanced tyer should take is to simply tie flies to imitate insects and describe them in that manner. How the tyer goes about assembling a "#14, dark grey, caddis dry fly" is irrelevant as long as it looks like a dark grey adult caddis, and is of the right size. This is the approach that we are going to take as we discuss the actual techniques for tying.

A pattern is simply a "recipe" for putting certain materials on the hook, in a certain manner. If the tyer knows the methods used, he can follow any recipe and tie virtually any pattern. More importantly, he can develop his own patterns to meet his need on the streams that he frequents—but *please,* we don't need any more *names* to add to the list.

Most flies are assembled using a tail, a body, wings, hackle, and a head. Some flies use only some of those parts and some will use all of them, so it is important that the tyer know as many different methods of tying each part as possible. We'll tackle each part of the fly assembly in a separate chapter and show you many ways of tying each. We'll also indicate what types of flies for which each method is best suited.

START WITH THE TAIL

The tail on the fly can serve many different purposes and, on some types it may serve more than one. On dry flies, the tail provides the support to float the heaviest part of the imitation: the bend area of the hook. In the case of many imitations, mayflies, stoneflies, some terrestrials, it also imitates the tail of the natural insect. In other cases, such as caddis fly imitations, the insect doesn't have a tail so we *only* have a tail on our imitation to provide support. On wet flies, we add a tail to imitate that part of the insect, to add animation, or, in some cases, both. The same holds true for nymphs. On most streamers, the tail is added so that it becomes a part of the wing to add bulk at the rear of the fly, just as a minnow's tail is wider than the body. The tail also adds some additional movement to the rear of the fly.

Hackle Tails. This is the most common tailing method for wet flies, nymphs, and dry flies, and is also seen on some streamer patterns. Really, it isn't a good tail for dry flies because capillary action will cause water to be drawn up between the hackle fibres and then the tail loses much of its ability to support the fly. It is used on many dry-fly patterns, but many of those patterns can be improved by selecting a better tailing method.

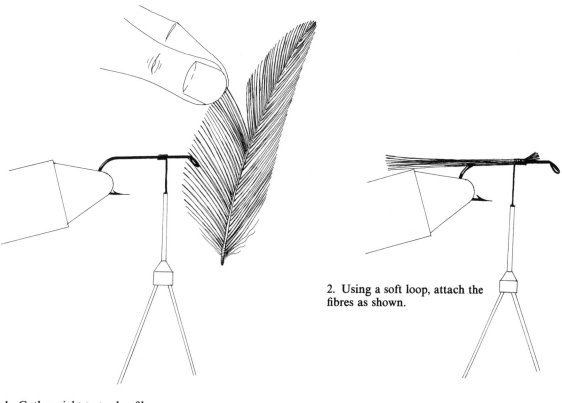

1. Gather eight to twelve fibres from a hackle and remove from the stem by pulling down and away from the stem. Be sure to grasp the fibres so that the ends are even in your fingers.

2. Using a soft loop, attach the fibres as shown.

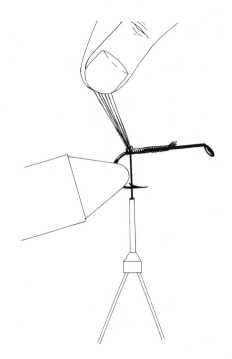

3. Wrap back on the fibres to a point directly opposite the barb of the hook. To keep the fibres on top of the hook, where they belong, hold the fibres angled slightly towards you and allow the tying thread to "carry" the fibres on top as you wrap. For dry flies, lift the tail up and take one turn of thread under the tail, then a soft turn over the top before continuing the thread forward. This anchors the tail firmly and will help to keep it from angling down as the fly is used.

The problem most people have with this tailing method is keeping the fibres on the top of the hook as they wrap. The trick here is to pull the fibres slightly towards you and allow the thread to position the fibres as you wrap. Keep in mind that you should select the fibres from a stiff, dry-fly hackle for tailing a dry fly, and from a soft hackle (hen hackle is great) for nymphs, streamers, and wet flies.

Calf-hair Tail. This is a good tailing technique which is used mostly on dry flies. Although the calf hair will have the same problem with capillarity as the hackle-fibre tail, the calf hair is stiffer and won't soften in the water as the hackle fibres will.

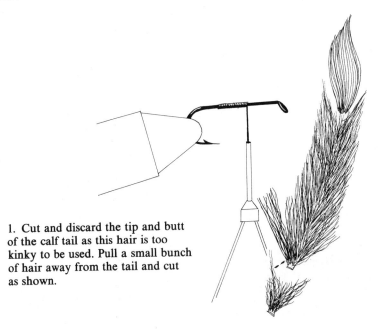

1. Cut and discard the tip and butt of the calf tail as this hair is too kinky to be used. Pull a small bunch of hair away from the tail and cut as shown.

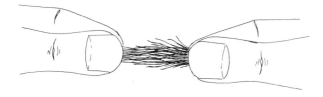

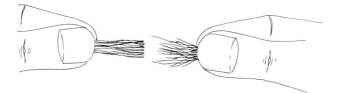

2. Hold the hair between the two hands as shown and pull all of the loose hair out with the left hand. Then grasp the remaining hair with the left hand and pull out all of the loose hair with the right hand. You should have the remaining bunch of evened hair in the left hand, holding the tips.

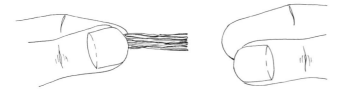

3. Tie the hair in at a point halfway between the point of the hook and the eye. Wrap back to a point directly opposite the barb. Use the same technique for keeping the hair on the top of the hook as you used for the hackle fibres: Hold the hair towards you as you wrap and allow the thread to position the hair on the top of the hook shank.

The only difficulty in dealing with a calf-hair tail is getting the hair evened. Because calf hair is so curly, it just won't even very well in a hair stacker so the method that we show here is used. To cover it again: Hold the bunch of hair in the right hand (by the butts) and pull out all loose fibres with the left hand. Then hold the tips in the left hand and pull out all of the loose fibres with the right. The remaining bunch will have the hair tips even. As a general rule, you will need to start with a bunch of hair two to three times as large as you want for the fly so that you'll have the right amount when you finish pulling the loose fibres out.

Goose-quill Tail. This type of tail is used almost exclusively on nymphal patterns. It is very representative of the wide tails found on some mayfly nymphs and the heavy tails seen on some stoneflies. Note that the section used is taken from the narrow (leading) edge of the goose quill, and that only one section of quill is used for each tail.

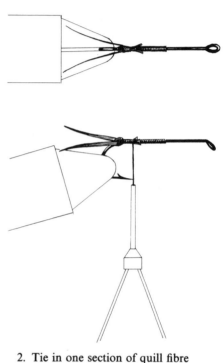

1. Form a small lump with your tying thread at a point directly opposite the barb of the hook. Cut two adjacent sections of quill from the narrow edge of the feather.

2. Tie in one section of quill fibre on each side of the hook, well behind the lump of thread as shown in the top view. Tie the sections in one at a time. Wrap the thread back to about the middle of the lump, making sure that the fibres stay positioned on the sides.

Notice that the fibres have a decided curve when removed from the feather: You will need to turn one of the fibres over so that each of them are curving away from the other for the tail to position correctly. The lump in the illustration is shown oversized so that you can better see what is going on; it should actually be about the size shown in step 2.

Forked-hair Tail. Javelina hair is most commonly used for this method of tailing but moose mane, woodchuck or rabbit whiskers, or even stripped-hackle quill may be used. This is an exceptionally good tail for use on dry flies as the wide spread of the tail acts as a stabilizer insuring that the fly floats upright. The tail is also usable and effective on some nymphal imitations.

66

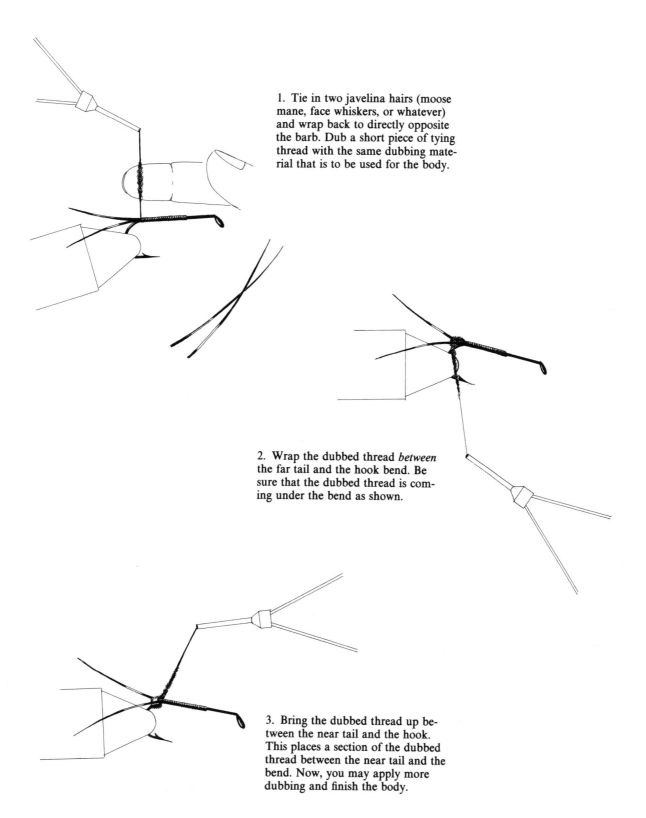

1. Tie in two javelina hairs (moose mane, face whiskers, or whatever) and wrap back to directly opposite the barb. Dub a short piece of tying thread with the same dubbing material that is to be used for the body.

2. Wrap the dubbed thread *between* the far tail and the hook bend. Be sure that the dubbed thread is coming under the bend as shown.

3. Bring the dubbed thread up between the near tail and the hook. This places a section of the dubbed thread between the near tail and the bend. Now, you may apply more dubbing and finish the body.

We use this type of tail on most of our dry flies because of the balancing provided by the tails and the lack of capillarity as with hackle-fibre tail.

67

Forked-hair Tail (alternate method). This method achieves the same result as the previously shown technique but isn't quite as easy to accomplish. The tails will have to be tied in individually, one side at a time, and it is harder to get a really smooth body shape from the lump of dubbing between the tails into the actual body. On the other hand, it is easier to get the tails spread wide with this method by simply increasing the size of the dubbed ball formed at the rear of the hook.

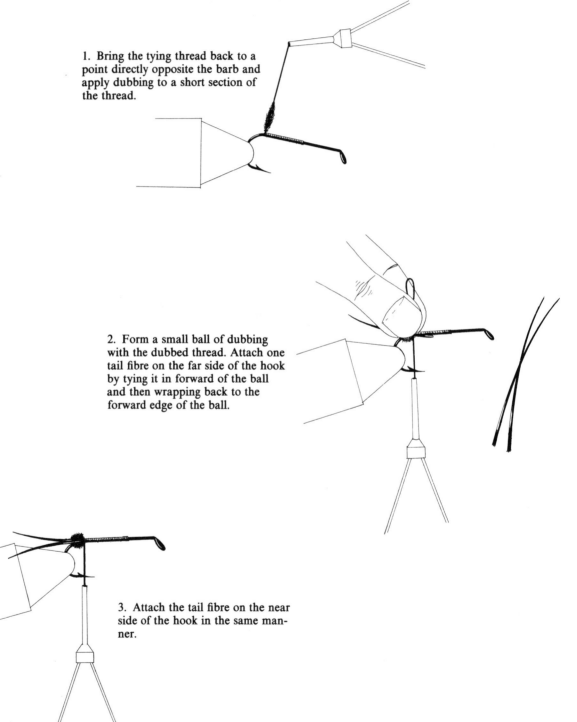

1. Bring the tying thread back to a point directly opposite the barb and apply dubbing to a short section of the thread.

2. Form a small ball of dubbing with the dubbed thread. Attach one tail fibre on the far side of the hook by tying it in forward of the ball and then wrapping back to the forward edge of the ball.

3. Attach the tail fibre on the near side of the hook in the same manner.

Hair Tail. The use of hair instead of hackle fibres for tails on dry flies is really an advantage when fishing fast, heavy water. The hair is naturally stiffer than hackle fibres, and the hair fibres are much more resistant to softening in the water. Hair tails are also used on wet flies, nymphs, and streamers.

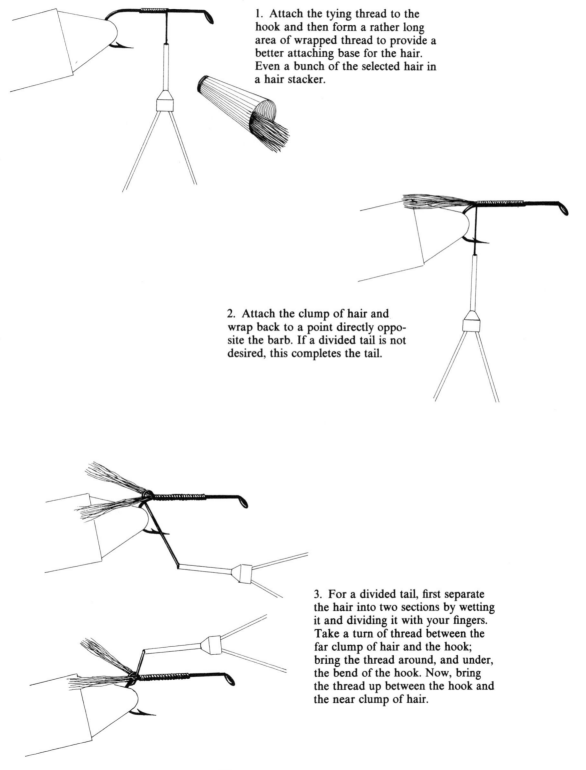

1. Attach the tying thread to the hook and then form a rather long area of wrapped thread to provide a better attaching base for the hair. Even a bunch of the selected hair in a hair stacker.

2. Attach the clump of hair and wrap back to a point directly opposite the barb. If a divided tail is not desired, this completes the tail.

3. For a divided tail, first separate the hair into two sections by wetting it and dividing it with your fingers. Take a turn of thread between the far clump of hair and the hook; bring the thread around, and under, the bend of the hook. Now, bring the thread up between the hook and the near clump of hair.

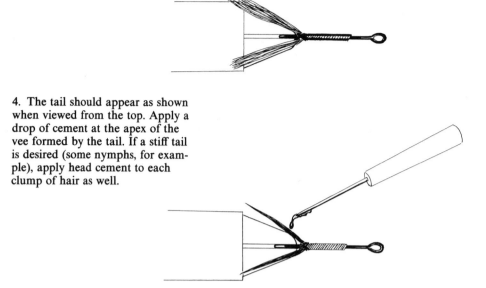

4. The tail should appear as shown when viewed from the top. Apply a drop of cement at the apex of the vee formed by the tail. If a stiff tail is desired (some nymphs, for example), apply head cement to each clump of hair as well.

Quill-section Tail. The Muddler Minnow and its variations are the main users of this tail type, but, since these are such popular types of flies, you should know how to accomplish the technique.

1. Cut a section from a quill as shown. Hold the section on the top of the hook shank and pinch the quill section and the hook shank firmly. Bring the tying thread up between the near side of the hook and the thumb and down between the far side and the finger. Hold the thread in a soft loop as shown. Pull firmly down on the thread. Repeat twice.

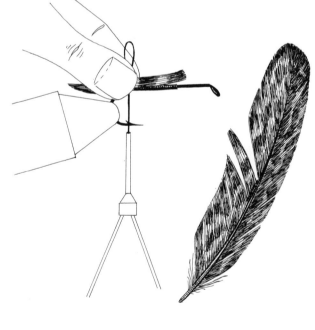

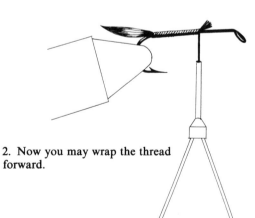

2. Now you may wrap the thread forward.

Once you have attached the quill section, the thread must *never* be wrapped any farther back than the original tie-in point.

six
Bodies

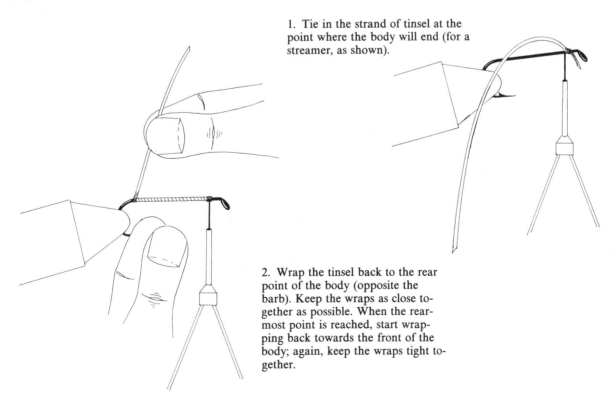

The number of materials and techniques that may be used to form the body of a fly are really unlimited so our approach will be to show you enough different methods to enable you to adapt one of them for any other material that you may want to use. As with all tying procedures, keep in mind that there are many different ways of accomplishing a given step in the tying process; we are simply showing what *we* consider the easiest way of going about it. If you find another method that works better for you, by all means use it!

Tinsel Body. Streamers are the flies that call for a tinsel body most often, although there are a few wet flies and dry flies that call for the use of tinsel as the entire body. We strongly recommend that you use the new Mylar® tinsels as they offer several advantages over the metallic tinsels: They are softer and easier to work with, they don't tend to cut the tying thread as metal tinsel does, and they won't tarnish. Flat tinsel is available in three sizes: 12, 14, and 16, with 12 being the largest (widest). You should have gold and silver in each of the sizes and use the smaller sizes as fly size decreases. Some companies make their flat Mylar® with gold on one side and silver on the other, which is a handy combination.

1. Tie in the strand of tinsel at the point where the body will end (for a streamer, as shown).

2. Wrap the tinsel back to the rear point of the body (opposite the barb). Keep the wraps as close together as possible. When the rearmost point is reached, start wrapping back towards the front of the body; again, keep the wraps tight together.

71

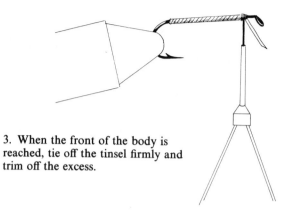

3. When the front of the body is reached, tie off the tinsel firmly and trim off the excess.

One thing that you need to watch for if using a double-sided Mylar® is that you will need to tie the tinsel in with the side that you want to show on the fly facing away from you. As you take the first wrap with the tinsel, it will have to turn 180°, putting the unseen side "up" on the fly.

Tubular Tinsel Body. This body type is used exclusively for streamers but it really is a good material for representing the flashy scales of a small bait-fish.

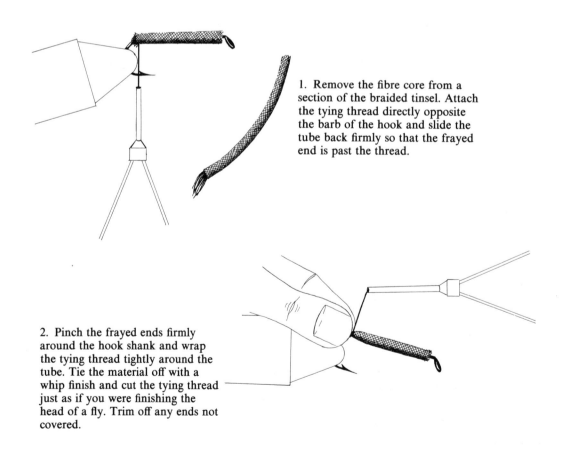

1. Remove the fibre core from a section of the braided tinsel. Attach the tying thread directly opposite the barb of the hook and slide the tube back firmly so that the frayed end is past the thread.

2. Pinch the frayed ends firmly around the hook shank and wrap the tying thread tightly around the tube. Tie the material off with a whip finish and cut the tying thread just as if you were finishing the head of a fly. Trim off any ends not covered.

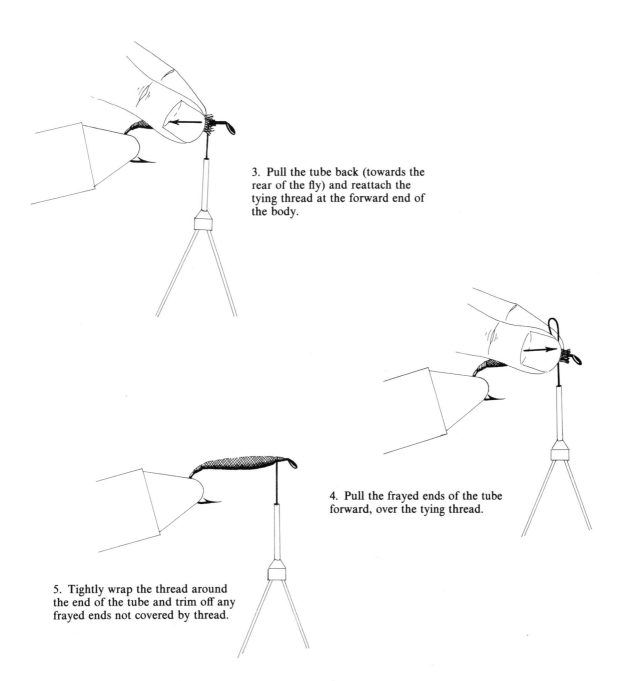

3. Pull the tube back (towards the rear of the fly) and reattach the tying thread at the forward end of the body.

4. Pull the frayed ends of the tube forward, over the tying thread.

5. Tightly wrap the thread around the end of the tube and trim off any frayed ends not covered by thread.

If a weighted streamer is desired, a piece of lead wire can be attached to the underside of the hook before the tube is slid on; this will also help to maintain the desired shape of the body. For an unweighted version, a piece of wooden matchstick can be added in the same manner.

Wire Body. Copper-, brass-, or silver-colored wire can be used for this body and it really is an efficient method for easily tying a weighted nymph or streamer. Note that the wire, in this case, is actually going to be the fly body; it gives good segmentation, a lot of "flash," and weights the fly, all in one operation.

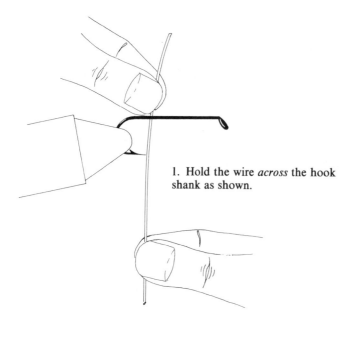

1. Hold the wire *across* the hook shank as shown.

2. Keeping the upper end of the wire firmly in position, begin wrapping the lower end of the wire as tightly around the hook shank as possible. Form a body in this manner to equal the desired body length. Cut both tag ends of the wire as close to the body as possible (use wire cutters).

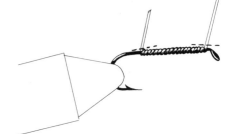

3. Slide the body back into the desired position. Attach the tying thread to the hook, just forward of the body, and then wrap back over the forward end of the wire. Wrap softly until the cut end of the wire is covered or the thread may be cut by the sharp end; then wrap firmly.

The one thing that you have to learn to judge is how long to make the body when it is forward, out of position. It is necessary to form the body on the forward end of the shank so that the point of the hook won't interfere with the wrapping of the wire.

Floss Body. This is one of the most commonly called for bodies on just about all of the fly types: dry flies, wet flies, nymphs, and streamers. It would appear to be about the easiest body to tie but, in reality, getting the proper body taper takes some attention.

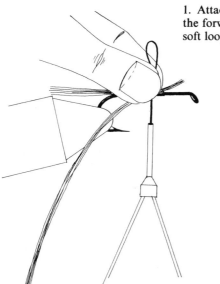

1. Attach the strand(s) of floss at the forward end of the body, using a soft loop.

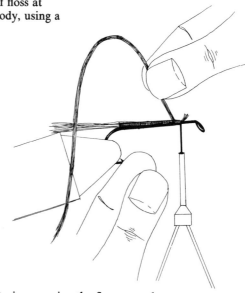

2. Begin wrapping the floss towards the rear of the hook. Notice that the fingers are kept very close to the hook at all times as the floss is wrapped.

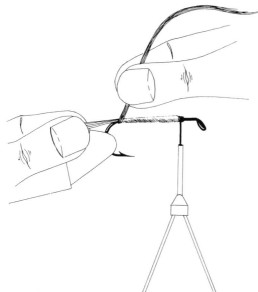

3. When the rear of the body is reached, hold the tail slightly towards you and allow the floss to carry it back into position as you start forward with the floss.

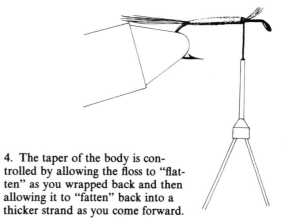

4. The taper of the body is controlled by allowing the floss to "flatten" as you wrapped back and then allowing it to "fatten" back into a thicker strand as you come forward.

There are really two tricks to handling floss: Keeping the fingers close to the hook shank as the floss is wrapped; and wetting the floss before handling it. This last point is important as it will make the floss easier to handle, will eliminate any tendency for the floss to fray as it passes through your fingers, and will allow you to see the color as it will appear once the fly is wet. Floss normally comes with four strands slightly twisted together; you should use the appropriate number of strands for the fly size you are tying—you don't *always* use all four strands!

Wool Body. Wool bodies are called for on quite a number of patterns; wool produces a body that is slightly fuzzier than a floss body. The best wool yarn that we have found for fly-tying is called crewel yarn and is available in most sewing shops. It comes as three strands twisted together and is easily separated so that you can use the appropriate number of strands for the size fly that you are tying. The real advantage, though, is that it is available in a very complete color range. Nice too, is the fact that it comes in small, 10-yard skeins that are easily stored and inexpensive.

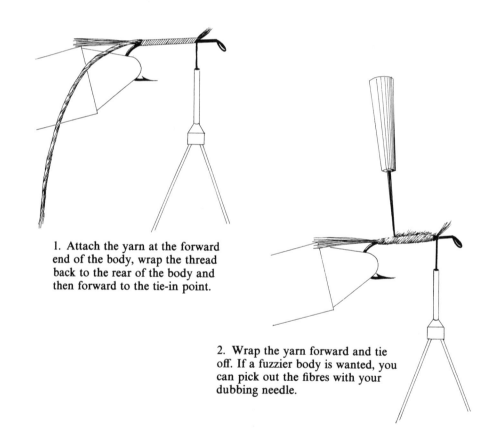

1. Attach the yarn at the forward end of the body, wrap the thread back to the rear of the body and then forward to the tie-in point.

2. Wrap the yarn forward and tie off. If a fuzzier body is wanted, you can pick out the fibres with your dubbing needle.

A slight taper can be added to the body by allowing the strands to flatten or fatten, much in the same manner as with floss but to a lesser degree. If a full-tapered body is desired, you will need to form the body shape with the tying thread before wrapping the yarn.

Chenille Body. Chenille provides the tyer with a quick and easy method for tying a fuzzy fly. It is available in several sizes, and the one used should be sized to the fly being tied.

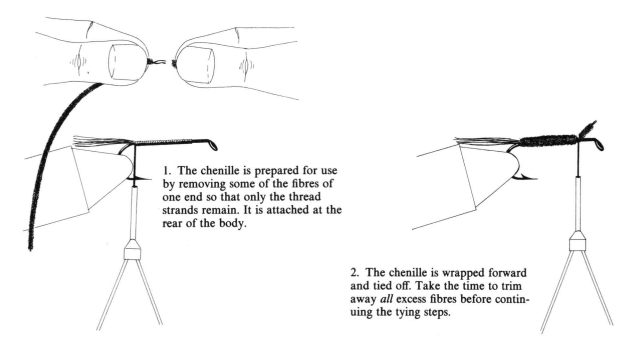

1. The chenille is prepared for use by removing some of the fibres of one end so that only the thread strands remain. It is attached at the rear of the body.

2. The chenille is wrapped forward and tied off. Take the time to trim away *all* excess fibres before continuing the tying steps.

The only way that you can get a tapered body using chenille is to form the taper with the tying thread before the chenille is wrapped.

Spun Dubbing. If you look back at the older, more traditional fly patterns, you will see that there weren't really that many that called for a dubbed body, whereas it seems that most of the newer patterns use this method for the body. The method that we show here is that used for most bodies calling for dubbing and works equally well with either natural fur or the new synthetics.

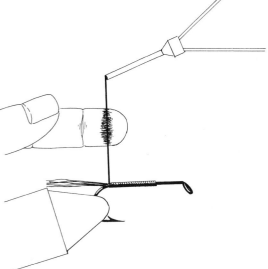

1. Spread a small patch of your selected dubbing on the thread with a finger (or two) as shown.

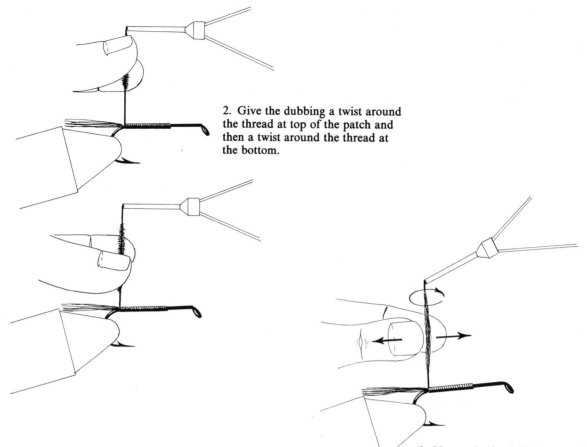

2. Give the dubbing a twist around the thread at top of the patch and then a twist around the thread at the bottom.

3. Now, spin the dubbing onto the thread by twisting the dubbing. Notice that the spinning motion is in only one direction.

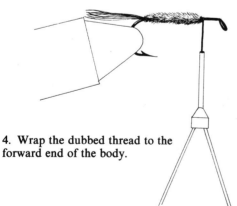

4. Wrap the dubbed thread to the forward end of the body.

Actually, in most cases, you will need to dub a section of thread and then wrap it, dub another section and wrap it, and so on until the full body length is reached. Don't try to apply too much material to the thread at a time.

78

Looped Thread Dubbing. This method of dubbing is normally used when a really shaggy body or thorax is needed on a particular imitation. This ragged appearance is achieved by dubbing the guard hairs in with the underfur. It is normally done using natural fur so that both types of material, guard hairs and underfur, are present.

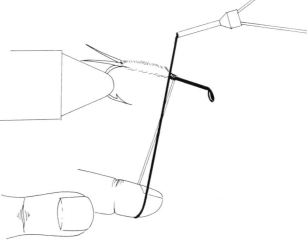

1. At the point where you wish the dubbed section to start, pull off a long loop of thread as shown and then wrap the thread over itself on the hook shank so that a separate loop is formed.

2. Hook a dubbing twister into the loop as shown (if you lack a dubbing twister, hackle pliers can be used). Cut a patch of fur and insert it into the loop as shown; applying some tension on the dubbing twister will hold the fur in position.

3. Keep applying additional fur until the loop is nearly full from top to bottom.

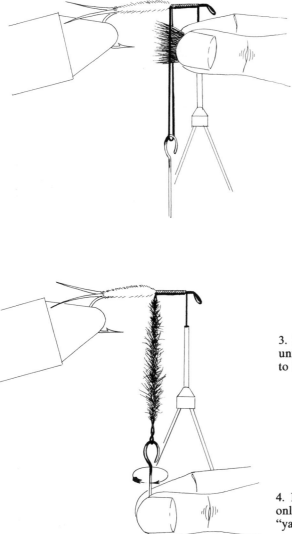

4. Now twist the loop (one direction only) until it is formed into a tight "yarn" of fur.

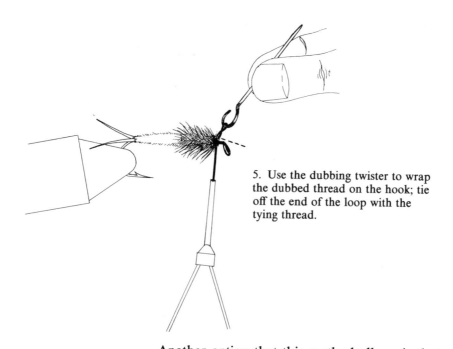

5. Use the dubbing twister to wrap the dubbed thread on the hook; tie off the end of the loop with the tying thread.

Another option that this method allows is that a thorax can be formed with dubbing and "hackled" with hair simultaneously. To do this, hold the twisted loop firmly and, with moistened fingers, stroke all of the guard hairs towards the rear of the fly. Now, when the loop is wrapped on the hook shank, the underfur will create a thorax and the guard hairs will form a nice "collar" at the forward end of the dubbed section.

Herl Body. There are a couple of tricks to getting a good, full body when using peacock or ostrich herl as a body material. One of these is to use several strands of herl. The other is to use this technique for wrapping the herl on the body.

1. Hold the tying thread above the hook at the point where you wish the body to begin. Twist the two or three strands of tied-in herl around the tying thread as shown.

2. Slide the fingers down the bobbin tube and grasp both the ends of the herl and the tying thread; note the position of the bobbin, which is cradled in the web between the finger and thumb.

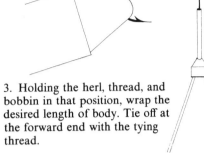

3. Holding the herl, thread, and bobbin in that position, wrap the desired length of body. Tie off at the forward end with the tying thread.

Moose-mane Body. This is the type of body that is used for the mosquito fly and some nymphs. Probably the most important point when using moose mane (and *all* stripped quill, as well) is to first soak the fibres before attempting to wrap them. This body uses two pieces of moose mane, a dark hair and a light hair which gives the finished body the distinctive light and dark segmentation.

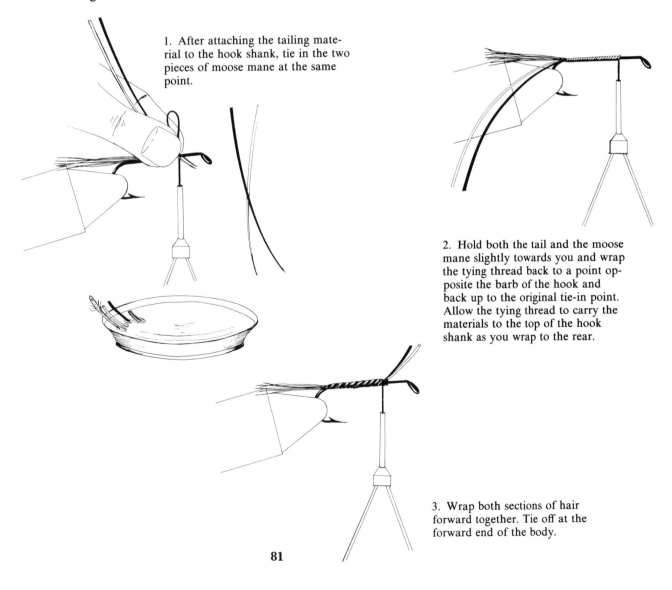

1. After attaching the tailing material to the hook shank, tie in the two pieces of moose mane at the same point.

2. Hold both the tail and the moose mane slightly towards you and wrap the tying thread back to a point opposite the barb of the hook and back up to the original tie-in point. Allow the tying thread to carry the materials to the top of the hook shank as you wrap to the rear.

3. Wrap both sections of hair forward together. Tie off at the forward end of the body.

When wrapping the two pieces of moose mane forward together, you must use your fingers instead of hackle pliers. One of the pieces of hair will invariably be thicker than the other and will shorten quicker as you wrap. By using your fingers, the piece that is wrapping faster can be allowed to slip through your fingers while still keeping tension on both pieces.

Hackle-stem Body. This is an easy, quick body to tie and results in a fly that has a nice segmented appearance. The stripped-hackle stem also has better durability than most quill-type bodies.

1. Strip all of the hackle fibres from the stem of the hackle and tie it in by the tip as shown.

2. Wrap the hackle stem forward and tie down with several tight turns of the thread.

By selecting from different colors of hackle, the tyer can get just about any body color that he desires. The natural taper of the hackle stem assures that the finished body will have a nice taper. Remember to soak the hackle stem before attempting to use it!

Stripped-peacock Herl. This is the body normally meant when a fly pattern calls for a quill body. The piece of herl should be selected from the eye of the peacock feather since these are the only fibres that have the desired light and dark coloring. This type of body is used on dry flies, wet flies, and nymphs.

1. Tie the section of stripped quill in by its tip. Normally, the quill section will not be long enough to tie it in the full length of the body; you will need to tie it in near the tail and then wrap the thread forward to the forward end of the body.

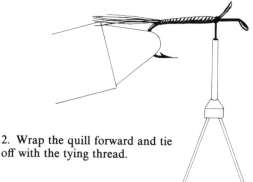

2. Wrap the quill forward and tie off with the tying thread.

There are many ways to strip the "fuzz" off the peacock quill so that the bare quill remains. It can be done with a fingernail or laid on the tying bench and stroked with a rubber eraser. Another method of stripping is to burn the fibres off by the use of household liquid bleach. This method is convenient but you must watch the process, or the bleach will completely dissolve the herl, quill and all. You can buy peacock eyes that have already been stripped or some suppliers offer wax-dipped eyes that you simply peel the wax from, taking the fuzz with it. One disadvantage of burning the fibres is that it will leave the quill very brittle. Wax, on the other hand, will leave the quill soft and ready to handle. Whatever the method used, the quill should be soaked before attempting to use it.

Spun-hair Body. Actually the spun-hair technique can be used on the head of the fly as well as the body, as on the Muddler Minnow. This technique really isn't difficult but it can be trying as you are learning. The best method that we have found to learn it is to forget about tying a fly that uses the method initially and just practice a few times on a bare hook.

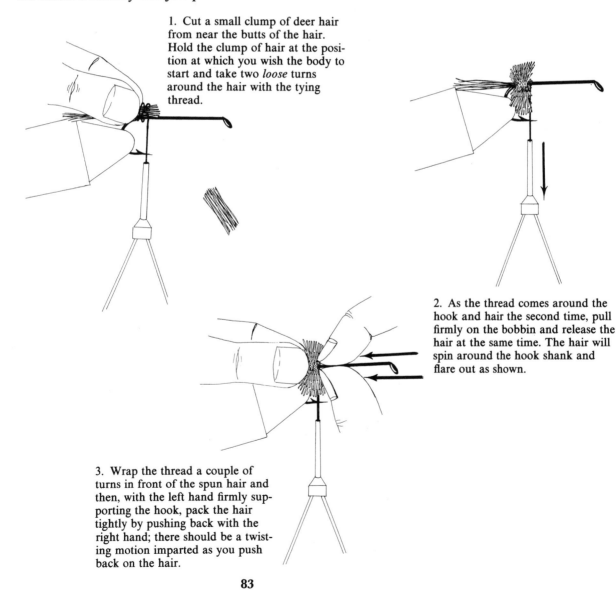

1. Cut a small clump of deer hair from near the butts of the hair. Hold the clump of hair at the position at which you wish the body to start and take two *loose* turns around the hair with the tying thread.

2. As the thread comes around the hook and hair the second time, pull firmly on the bobbin and release the hair at the same time. The hair will spin around the hook shank and flare out as shown.

3. Wrap the thread a couple of turns in front of the spun hair and then, with the left hand firmly supporting the hook, pack the hair tightly by pushing back with the right hand; there should be a twisting motion imparted as you push back on the hair.

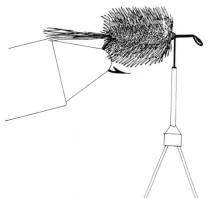

4. Keep spinning on additional sections of hair (remember to pack each one tightly) until the forward end of the body is reached. The shaping of the body will be much easier if you remove the hook from the vise, so tie off with a whip finish and cut the thread loose.

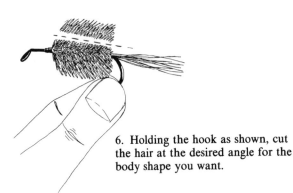

5. Hold the hook by the eye and trim off the hair to form a smooth collar at the rear; be careful that you don't cut the tail off!

6. Holding the hook as shown, cut the hair at the desired angle for the body shape you want.

7. Reverse the hook in the fingers and cut the hair on the bottom to the desired shape.

8. Hold the hook firmly between the thumb and finger (flatten the hair) and cut the hair from one side. Turn the hook upside down in the fingers, flatten the hair again, and trim off the other side. Don't get overly concerned about really getting the cuts smooth as we'll take care of that in the next step.

9. Hold the hook in the left hand (note that the fingers are covering and protecting the tail) and, with a match, begin singeing the hair into shape. The match should be kept moving all the time. You will notice that the hair seems to melt away from the match, and you will quickly learn to control this so that you can shape the hair quickly and easily.

Spun hair is the best method that the fly tyer has of adding a great deal of bulk to the fly without adding a lot of extra weight, making it ideal for dry flies and some streamers. It is particularly good for dry flies as the hair is hollow, aiding its floating qualities. Deer hair is the material normally called for and used, but any of the hollow hairs can be used. Antelope, elk, and caribou are all suitable. After you have mastered the technique of releasing the hair *just* as you tighten the thread to spin the hair, the rest is pretty easy. Don't neglect to work at really packing each bunch of spun hair tightly before adding the next bunch. The match method of shaping the spun hair is, by far, the fastest and easiest but be careful to: cover the things you don't want singed with your fingers; keep the match moving; and, above all, don't make the mistake of moving the match under the fly to shape the bottom; turn the fly over and continue to use the bottom edge of the flame.

Stripped-quill Body. A section peeled from the center stem of a duck or goose quill is used for the body shown here. Peel all of the feather fibres from the stem and soak it before attempting to strip the section from the stem. This really makes an attractive quill body and is a little-used technique.

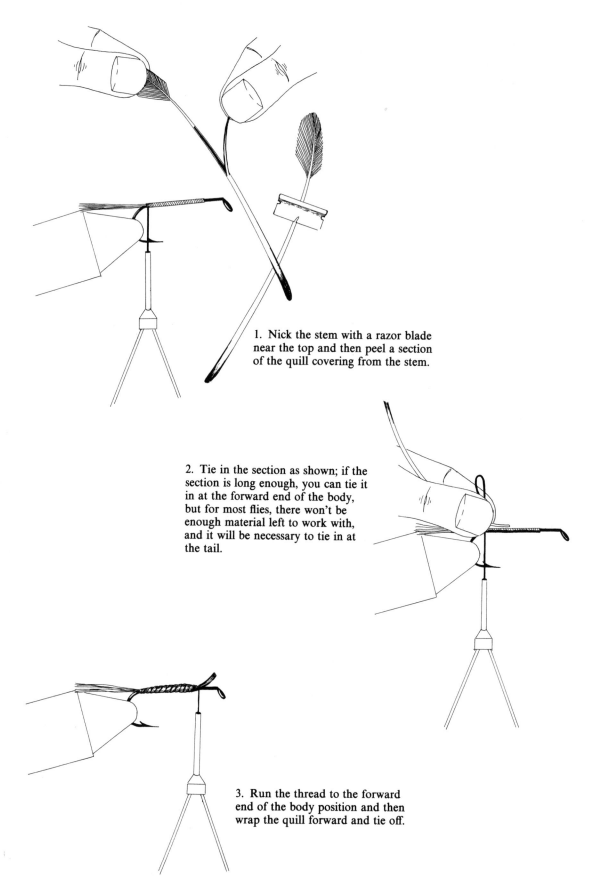

1. Nick the stem with a razor blade near the top and then peel a section of the quill covering from the stem.

2. Tie in the section as shown; if the section is long enough, you can tie it in at the forward end of the body, but for most flies, there won't be enough material left to work with, and it will be necessary to tie in at the tail.

3. Run the thread to the forward end of the body position and then wrap the quill forward and tie off.

This method gives the body good segmentation, is durable, and, because the peeled section is naturally tapered, builds a tapered body.

Swannundaze®. This is a really neat material that lends itself well to the tying of nymph and streamer bodies. It is a synthetic material that is formed in a flat oval and is available in a great number of colors in three different sizes.

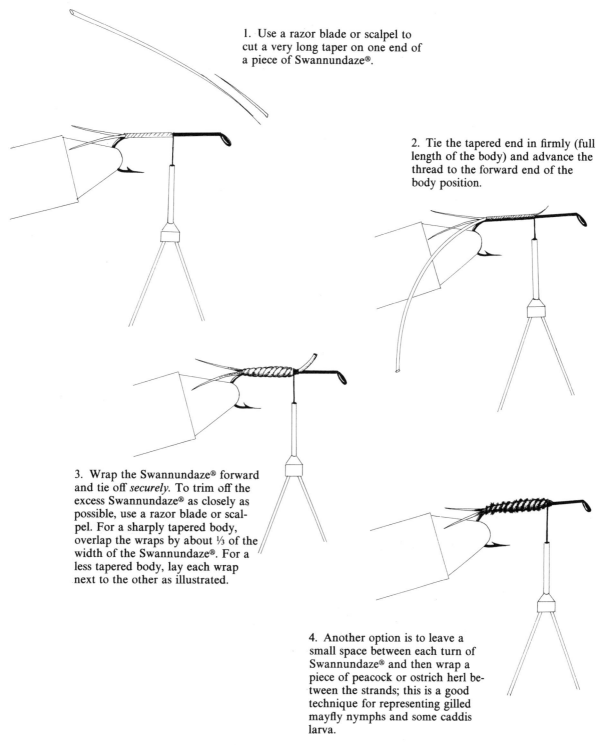

1. Use a razor blade or scalpel to cut a very long taper on one end of a piece of Swannundaze®.

2. Tie the tapered end in firmly (full length of the body) and advance the thread to the forward end of the body position.

3. Wrap the Swannundaze® forward and tie off *securely*. To trim off the excess Swannundaze® as closely as possible, use a razor blade or scalpel. For a sharply tapered body, overlap the wraps by about ⅓ of the width of the Swannundaze®. For a less tapered body, lay each wrap next to the other as illustrated.

4. Another option is to leave a small space between each turn of Swannundaze® and then wrap a piece of peacock or ostrich herl between the strands; this is a good technique for representing gilled mayfly nymphs and some caddis larva.

Deer-hair Body. This body type is really a floater: the hair used is hollow and, in the act of tying, we bind down both ends of the hair so that each hair contains a hollow chamber. The rather bulky body that results is very good for use on some of the terrestrials, such as, inch worms, grasshoppers, and crickets.

1. Tie in a bunch of deer hair by the tips. The bulkiness of the finished body will be determined by the size of the bunch of hair that you tie in during this step.

2. Run the tying thread back to a point opposite the barb of the hook and back up to where the body will end.

3. Fold the bunch of hair forward and tie down, cinching it tightly.

4. Now, wrap the thread to the back of the body in a widely spaced spiral, and then back up to the front of the body. Trim off any excess hair.

The spiraling of the thread over the length of the body is important as deer hair is pretty soft and the trout's teeth will quickly cut it. By wrapping it in this manner, the body will still be held intact even though some of the fibres may be cut.

Deer-hair Body (*humpy style*). This method will, at first, appear to be the same as the one we just covered but when we get to the end you'll see that there is really quite a difference in the finished product.

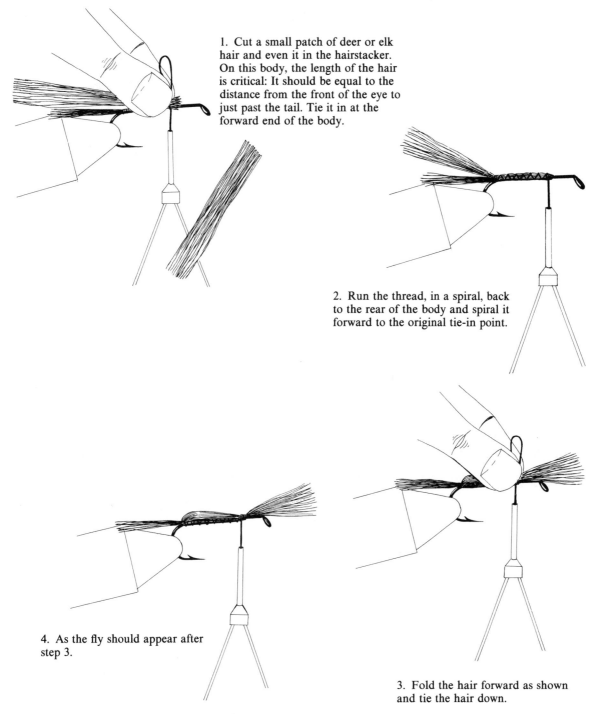

1. Cut a small patch of deer or elk hair and even it in the hairstacker. On this body, the length of the hair is critical: It should be equal to the distance from the front of the eye to just past the tail. Tie it in at the forward end of the body.

2. Run the thread, in a spiral, back to the rear of the body and spiral it forward to the original tie-in point.

4. As the fly should appear after step 3.

3. Fold the hair forward as shown and tie the hair down.

5. Pull the hair up and back with the left hand and take enough turns of thread in front of the hair to hold it in the upright position.

6. Now, with your fingers divide the hair into two even sections.

7. Take a couple of turns around the base of each wing with the tying thread and add a drop of lacquer to each wing base.

How about that? You not only tied a nice-looking deer-hair body but managed to come out of it with an attractive divided wing. Now you can see why the initial measurement of the deer hair was so important; if that measurement isn't right, your wing will be too tall or too short to be in proper proportion.

Latex Body. This is a nice technique to use for imitating the smooth-bodied caddis larva. Typically, they have a "rubbery" appearance with prominent segmentation.

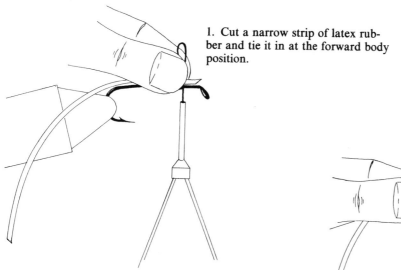

1. Cut a narrow strip of latex rubber and tie it in at the forward body position.

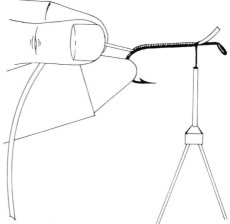

2. Stretch the rubber strip back and wrap the thread to the rear of the hook and back forward to the tie-in point.

3. If a bulky body is wanted, shape the body with wool yarn or other material as shown.

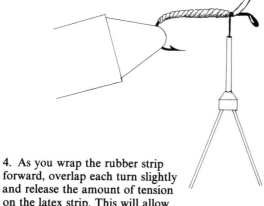

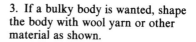

4. As you wrap the rubber strip forward, overlap each turn slightly and release the amount of tension on the latex strip. This will allow the latex to thicken and result in a natural-appearing tapered body.

Porcupine-quill Extended Body. Here's a really old method of tying an extended mayfly body that is kind of fun and works well too.

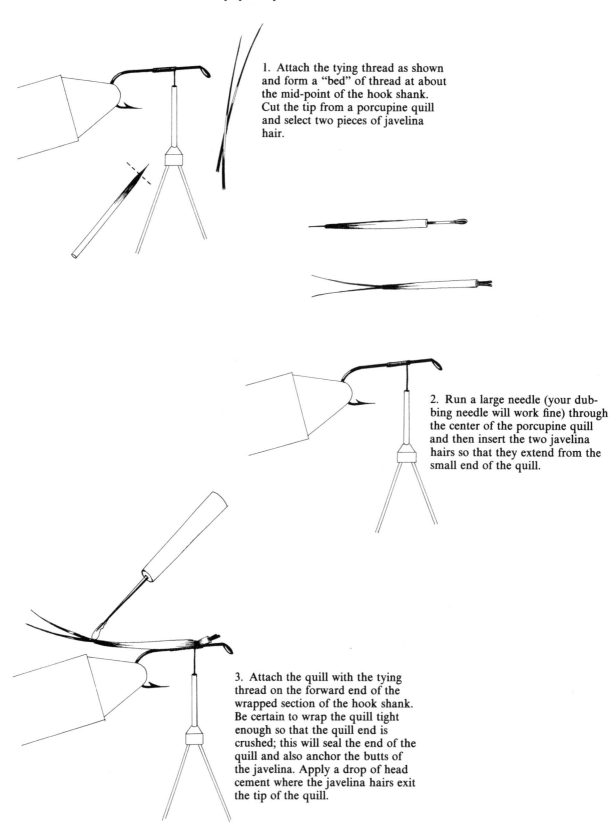

1. Attach the tying thread as shown and form a "bed" of thread at about the mid-point of the hook shank. Cut the tip from a porcupine quill and select two pieces of javelina hair.

2. Run a large needle (your dubbing needle will work fine) through the center of the porcupine quill and then insert the two javelina hairs so that they extend from the small end of the quill.

3. Attach the quill with the tying thread on the forward end of the wrapped section of the hook shank. Be certain to wrap the quill tight enough so that the quill end is crushed; this will seal the end of the quill and also anchor the butts of the javelina. Apply a drop of head cement where the javelina hairs exit the tip of the quill.

Thread Body (Ant). This is about the easiest method for forming the typical ant shape.

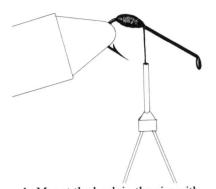

1. Mount the hook in the vise with the shank tipped down as shown. If you are using a vise that will allow you to tip the jaws, you can mount the hook normally and then just tip the vise down to get this hook position. Form a ball of tying thread around the upper part of the bend of the hook. Make each wrap of thread tight so that the thread won't unpile as you build the ball.

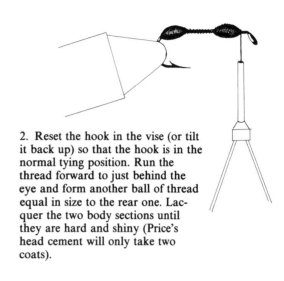

2. Reset the hook in the vise (or tilt it back up) so that the hook is in the normal tying position. Run the thread forward to just behind the eye and form another ball of thread equal in size to the rear one. Lacquer the two body sections until they are hard and shiny (Price's head cement will only take two coats).

One alternative here is to make the two body parts of different colors of thread, normally red and black, if you need to imitate some of the ants that are colored like that.

Extended Mayfly Body. The one thing that is rather unique about this body type is that the body is constructed independently of the rest of the fly. Any of the hollow hairs may be used, but the texture of elk hair seems to be the easiest to work with.

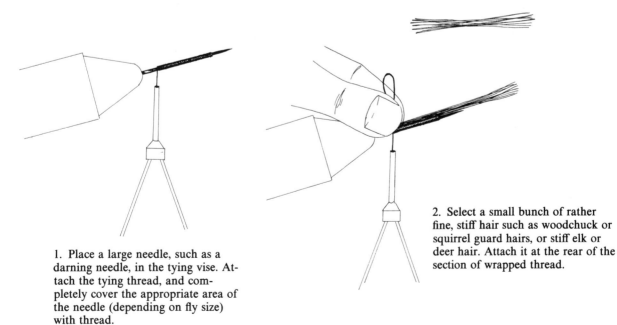

1. Place a large needle, such as a darning needle, in the tying vise. Attach the tying thread, and completely cover the appropriate area of the needle (depending on fly size) with thread.

2. Select a small bunch of rather fine, stiff hair such as woodchuck or squirrel guard hairs, or stiff elk or deer hair. Attach it at the rear of the section of wrapped thread.

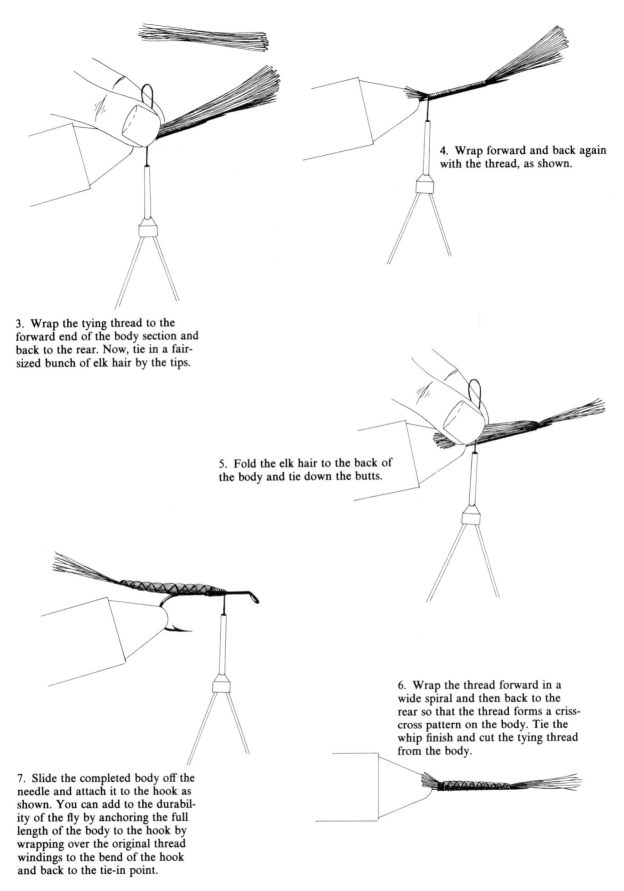

3. Wrap the tying thread to the forward end of the body section and back to the rear. Now, tie in a fair-sized bunch of elk hair by the tips.

4. Wrap forward and back again with the thread, as shown.

5. Fold the elk hair to the back of the body and tie down the butts.

6. Wrap the thread forward in a wide spiral and then back to the rear so that the thread forms a criss-cross pattern on the body. Tie the whip finish and cut the tying thread from the body.

7. Slide the completed body off the needle and attach it to the hook as shown. You can add to the durability of the fly by anchoring the full length of the body to the hook by wrapping over the original thread windings to the bend of the hook and back to the tie-in point.

This type of body lends itself very well to continuing the fly to completion by using cut or burnt wings and a parachute hackle. As with all extended bodies, the fly will eventually hinge at the point where the body leaves the hook and becomes useless. For those times when you really need to be imitative of the adult mayfly, though, they will really do the trick.

Reversed Ribbed Body. This is a great body for representing any of the smooth-bodied caddis larvae. The whole appearance of the fly changes when we add the wire ribbing under the floss instead of over it as usual.

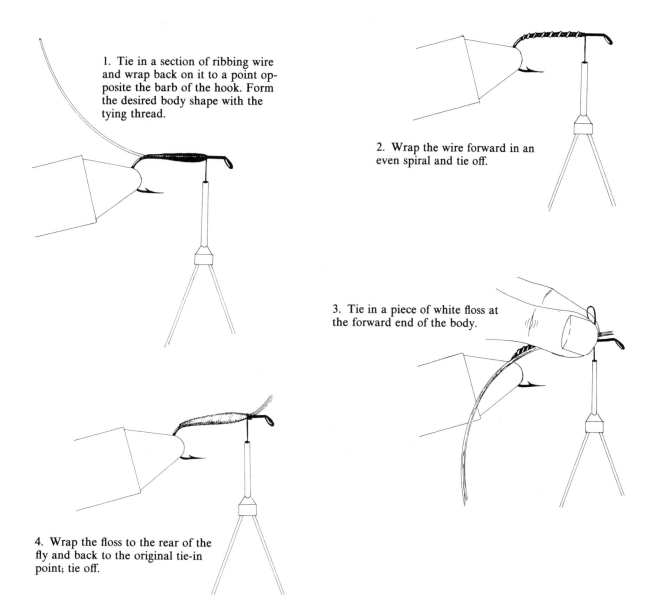

1. Tie in a section of ribbing wire and wrap back on it to a point opposite the barb of the hook. Form the desired body shape with the tying thread.

2. Wrap the wire forward in an even spiral and tie off.

3. Tie in a piece of white floss at the forward end of the body.

4. Wrap the floss to the rear of the fly and back to the original tie-in point; tie off.

The best thing about this fly is that it is so simple to tie, and yet, can represent any of the smooth-bodied caddis larvae. The secret is in selecting the thread color. Once the white floss is wet, it becomes almost transparent, and if you've used black thread, the fly will take on a nice grey color. If you use orange thread, the fly will show as a rusty brown when wet; and if you use green thread, the fly will be olive when wet. The ribbing under the floss provides the needed segmentation without giving any bright flash that would be unnatural for a caddis larva.

RIBBING

Ribbing is added to a fly for any of several reasons: To add some "flash" to the fly; to provide segmentation to the body, or to strengthen the underlying materials. In some instances, you may use ribbing to get all three of the benefits in one fly. One of the best things that has happened for the fly tyer is the introduction of Mylar® tinsel in the market. Metallic tinsel is stiff and rather hard to handle, it has sharp edges that can cut the tying thread, and it tarnishes unless covered with lacquer. Mylar® overcomes all of these difficulties.

The use of wire as a ribbing material is becoming more and more common. The wire normally used is called beading wire and is available in any craft shop in either gold or silver.

Thread Ribbing. Using the thread as the ribbing material has the advantage of not requiring the tyer to attach another material to the hook, it looks good, and it is pretty durable.

1. The ribbing is prepared by leaving a loop of tying thread at the rear of the body. This is accomplished by pulling some extra thread from the bobbin and then wrapping over the ends on the hook. Any type of body material could now be added.

2. Fold the wing case forward and tie down. Wrap the doubled strand of thread forward in a spiral and tie off at the forward end of the body.

In this case, we were using a section of quill as the wing case and since quill is a rather fragile material, the thread ribbing was used to help protect it. If a finer ribbing is wanted, such as on a small fly, one end of the thread loop could have been cut where the loop leaves the body, leaving you with a single strand of thread.

Quill Ribbing. Generally when a quill ribbing is called for, a stripped hackle stem can be substituted with advantage. As we just said, quills (peacock, ostrich, wing quill, etc.) tend to be rather fragile and really aren't very well suited for use as ribbing. The stripped hackle stem is much more durable. In any case, whether quill or hackle stem is used, make sure it is well soaked before tying it in.

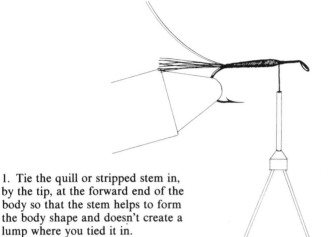

1. Tie the quill or stripped stem in, by the tip, at the forward end of the body so that the stem helps to form the body shape and doesn't create a lump where you tied it in.

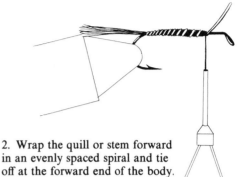

2. Wrap the quill or stem forward in an evenly spaced spiral and tie off at the forward end of the body.

Tinsel Ribbing. Nothing really difficult here, just make sure that you cut the end of the tinsel that you are tying in so that it has a fairly long taper to it.

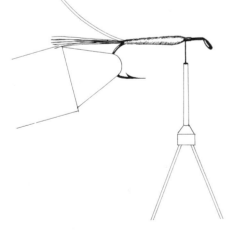

1. Tie in the tinsel first so that it lies under the full length of the body.

2. Wrap the tinsel forward in an even spiral, keeping the wraps as tight as possible.

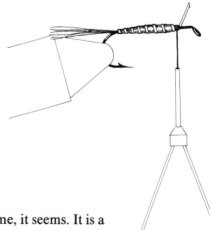

Wire Ribbing. Wire is becoming more popular all the time, it seems. It is a good ribbing material, particularly on wet flies and nymphs where the weight that it adds aids in sinking the fly.

1. As with all of the ribbings, tie the wire in at the forward end of the body so that it lays under the full length so that no lumps are seen where you tied it in.

2. Wrap the wire forward tightly and tie off at the forward end of the body.

WEIGHTING

Many times, it is desired to have a wet fly, nymph, or streamer that is heavier than can be achieved, using only the materials called for in the pattern. Lead wire is then added to the fly, under the body, so that the fly will sink faster and stay in the lower reaches of the stream.

Bottom Weighting. In this technique, the weight is added to the underside of the hook. By attaching the lead wire in this manner, the tyer is assured that the hook will ride upright in the water. This method of the wire also aids in establishing the desired body shape for minnow patterns.

1. Mount the hook in the vise with the point up or, if using a vise that has a rotating head, mount the hook normally and rotate it to the inverted position. Hold the lead wire (1 or 2 sections, as desired) on the bottom of the shank and anchor with the tying thread. Strips should be cut equal to the body length.

2. Completely cover the lead wire with the thread, being particularly careful to completely cover the ends of the wire.

Lead wire used for weighting is available from most fly shops and catalogue order suppliers. If you want to save some money over the long term, you can buy the wire in bulk at your local electrical shop: it is called fuse wire and comes in a wide range of sizes.

Lead-strip Weighting. This method of weighting is used, primarily, for those flies that are representative of the freshwater shrimps or scuds. The materials used are the same lead strips that nymph fishermen use for wrap-on weight. The arched lead achieves the typical humped body shape for these types of imitations and, since the weight is on the top side of the hook shank, the fly will ride in the water with the hook up, making it almost weedless.

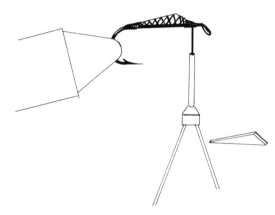

1. Cut a section of lead strip in a triangular shape as shown; be sure to cut the ends in a rather long taper. Attach it to the top of the hook shank by first anchoring the back (thin) end, and then spiraling the thread to the front and anchoring that end. Now, wrap from the front to back and forward again several times to firmly anchor the lead in position.

Side-wire Weighting. Many of the aquatic insects have a flattened shape in the abdominal area. This method of weighting helps to arrive at the desired shape and also lets us add considerable weight to the fly because we are adding a strip of wire to each side.

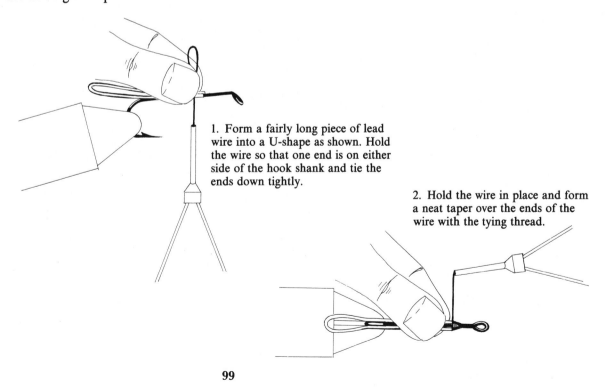

1. Form a fairly long piece of lead wire into a U-shape as shown. Hold the wire so that one end is on either side of the hook shank and tie the ends down tightly.

2. Hold the wire in place and form a neat taper over the ends of the wire with the tying thread.

3. Wrap back on the hook and wire, holding the wire in position on either side of the hook. When you get close to the rear of the body, cut the U from the wire and trim the ends to the proper length for the body.

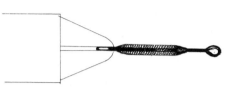

4. Continue wrapping back on the hook, holding the wire in position until the wire is attached the full length of the body. Form a neat taper over the rear ends of the wire and wrap the body from end to end tightly with the tying thread.

Wrapped-wire Body. This is the simplest method of weighting a fly and offers the added advantage of being the method that lets us get the most weight on a fly. The method used is essentially the same as that used for making a wire-bodied fly.

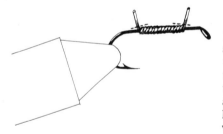

1. Hold the wire across the hook shank at the position where you wish the body to begin. Holding the upper end firmly, begin wrapping the wire around the body as tightly as possible. When the desired body length is reached, trim off the excess wire with wire cutters.

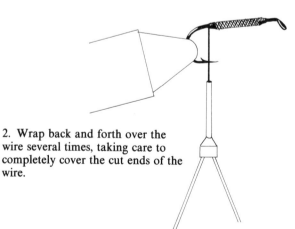

2. Wrap back and forth over the wire several times, taking care to completely cover the cut ends of the wire.

seven
Wings and Wing Cases

The wing may perform several different functions on a fly. In the cases where we are actually representing an insect, the wing is the most important part of the imitation as far as presenting the correct silhouette. On both wet flies and dry flies the wing is meant to be imitative of the actual wing found on the insect. On nymphal imitations, the wing case is meant to represent the actual body part of the insect. The wing on streamers, on the other hand, isn't really a wing at all; it is used as part of the body silhouette of the bait-fish imitation and serves the additional role of providing the bulk of the movement of the fly. Because the wing type is so easily identified with a particular type of fly, they are easily grouped by their intended use and we will present them in that manner. In the few cases where a particular wing type may be used for more than one fly style, we will mention that point.

WET-FLY WINGS

Quill Wing. This is the most common type of wing found on wet flies and is probably effective because it results in general shape of the wing on an emerging insect. As with all quill wings, this one is rather fragile and just won't stand up to a lot of hard use. You can offset this problem to some degree by spraying the quill sections with a substance called Tuffilm®. Tuffilm® is available in any art supply store, it comes in a spray can and its intended use is for fixing charcoal and pastel drawings.

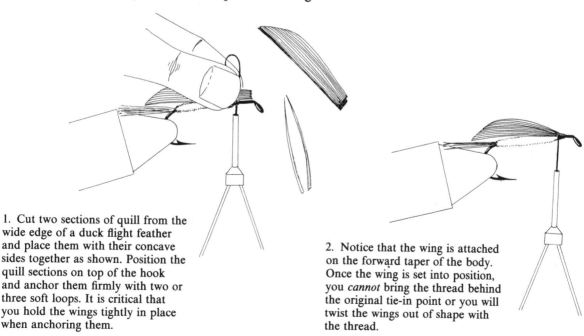

1. Cut two sections of quill from the wide edge of a duck flight feather and place them with their concave sides together as shown. Position the quill sections on top of the hook and anchor them firmly with two or three soft loops. It is critical that you hold the wings tightly in place when anchoring them.

2. Notice that the wing is attached on the forward taper of the body. Once the wing is set into position, you *cannot* bring the thread behind the original tie-in point or you will twist the wings out of shape with the thread.

101

Hair Wing. The hair-wing wet fly is much more durable than the quill-wing type and is just as representative of the emerging insect shape.

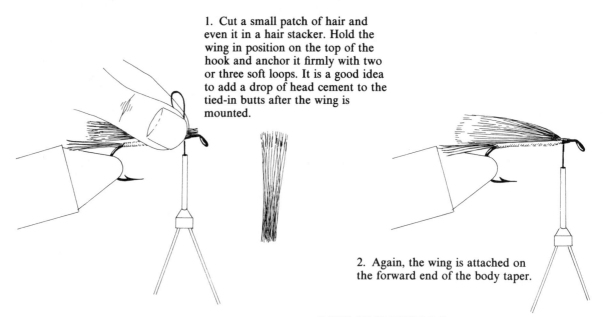

1. Cut a small patch of hair and even it in a hair stacker. Hold the wing in position on the top of the hook and anchor it firmly with two or three soft loops. It is a good idea to add a drop of head cement to the tied-in butts after the wing is mounted.

2. Again, the wing is attached on the forward end of the body taper.

DRY-FLY WINGS

Quill Wing. This was, for many years, the most common type of wing seen on dry flies. It does provide a pretty good silhouette for the imitation of the adult mayfly but it has several drawbacks. It isn't the easiest of the wing types to assemble, it tends to twist the leader as it is cast, and it lacks durability. Because of these disadvantages, it is seen less frequently on the stream. The manner of tying is much the same as for the quill-wing wet fly but there are a few important differences, as we will see.

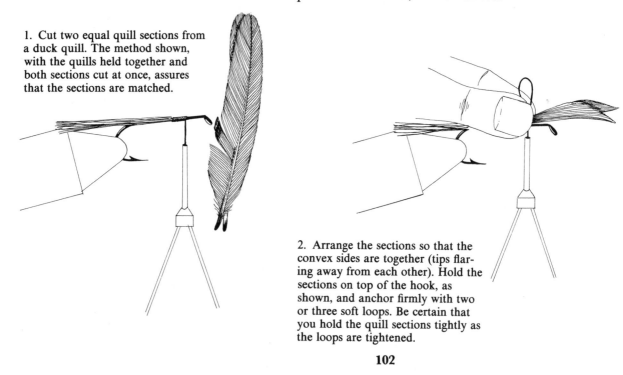

1. Cut two equal quill sections from a duck quill. The method shown, with the quills held together and both sections cut at once, assures that the sections are matched.

2. Arrange the sections so that the convex sides are together (tips flaring away from each other). Hold the sections on top of the hook, as shown, and anchor firmly with two or three soft loops. Be certain that you hold the quill sections tightly as the loops are tightened.

3. Grasp the wing sections near the tips and pull them back slightly past vertical. Take several turns of thread in front of the wing bases to hold the wings in position.

4. The completed wing.

Hackle-tip Wing. The hackle-tip wing is seen frequently on dry flies and is a good choice as it provides a good silhouette of the adult mayfly and is considerably more durable than the quill wing. The hackle selected for the wing should be rather soft, with a lot of web, so that the wing is presented as a more solid form.

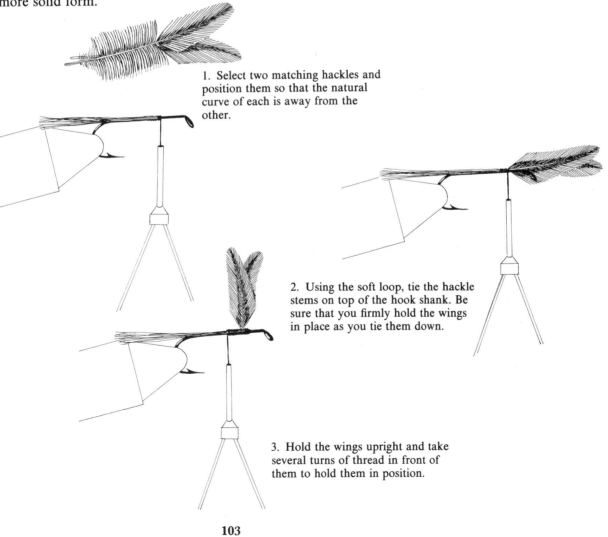

1. Select two matching hackles and position them so that the natural curve of each is away from the other.

2. Using the soft loop, tie the hackle stems on top of the hook shank. Be sure that you firmly hold the wings in place as you tie them down.

3. Hold the wings upright and take several turns of thread in front of them to hold them in position.

Rolled Wing. The rolled wing provides a good mayfly silhouette, is fairly durable, and has the added advantage of using material that is marked to give a hint of the veining found in the natural wing of the insect. Mallard, teal, or wood duck body feathers are used.

1. Cut the center stem of the feather so as to remove a section as shown.

2. Tie the feather in (using the soft loop again) with the tips out over the eye of the hook.

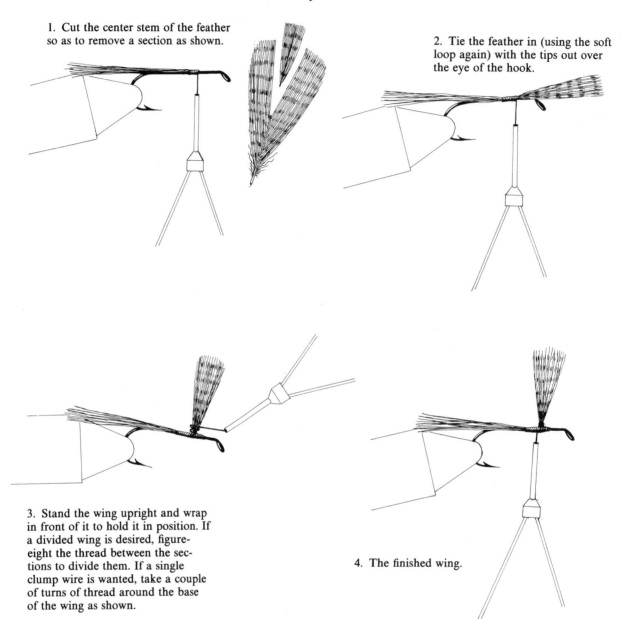

3. Stand the wing upright and wrap in front of it to hold it in position. If a divided wing is desired, figure-eight the thread between the sections to divide them. If a single clump wire is wanted, take a couple of turns of thread around the base of the wing as shown.

4. The finished wing.

Hair Wing (Downwing style). This style of hair wing is used to imitate the adult stoneflies and adult caddis flies which, unlike the mayflies, carry their wings back over their body. Materials most commonly used are elk hair, deer hair, badger, and squirrel. This style of wing not only imitates the actual insect's wing, but also helps to support the fly on the water.

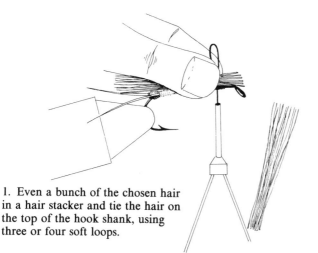

1. Even a bunch of the chosen hair in a hair stacker and tie the hair on the top of the hook shank, using three or four soft loops.

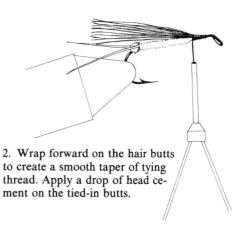

2. Wrap forward on the hair butts to create a smooth taper of tying thread. Apply a drop of head cement on the tied-in butts.

Hair Wing (*Upright style*). This is the most durable of the mayfly wings. It provides a good silhouette, and is fairly easy to tie. If there is any disadvantage to the upright hair wing, it is that it is rather bulky at the tie-in point, which becomes of importance when tying really small flies. Calf tail and bucktail are the most commonly used materials, although elk hair and deer hair can be used. Calf tail is the only hair of these that can't be evened in a hair stacker, so we are showing the method used for working with calf tail.

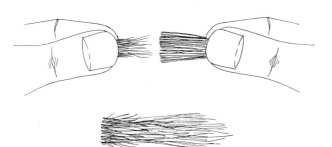

1. To prepare the calf tail (cut bunch shown in center), hold the tips and with the left hand, pull out all of the short hairs. Grasp the remaining hair by the butts and pull out any loose hairs with the right hand.

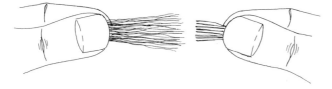

2. Hold the bunch of evened hair in position on the top of the hook shank and anchor with three or four soft loops.

105

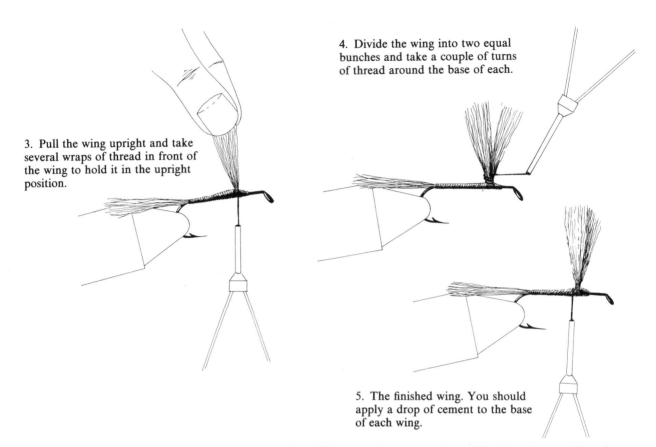

3. Pull the wing upright and take several wraps of thread in front of the wing to hold it in the upright position.

4. Divide the wing into two equal bunches and take a couple of turns of thread around the base of each.

5. The finished wing. You should apply a drop of cement to the base of each wing.

Burnt or Cut Wing. The use of a cut section of feather for upright wings on dry flies isn't anything new but with the advent of wing burners, there has been a resurgence of interest in their use. The cutting of two, perfectly equal, wing sections is difficult and, undoubtedly, had a lot to do with the fact that cut-wing flies weren't too popular; the wing burners now make the wing preparation an easy task.

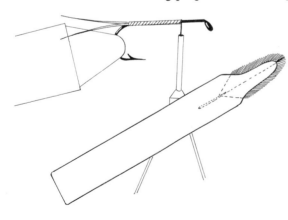

1. Place the feather to be used in the wing former and, holding the wing former tightly closed, use a match or lighter to burn away any material extending from the edges. Note that there is a long section of hackle stem still attached to the feather.

2. Tie the hackle stems in on the top of the hook shank (just as for the hackle-tip wing), pull the wing upright and wrap in front to hold it in place.

Burnt Wing (Fly-Rite® Poly II). The use of polypropylene sheet material for the wing requires a bit more time but results in a wing that is practically indestructible.

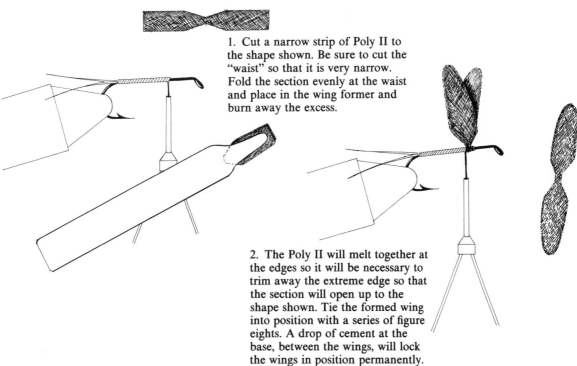

1. Cut a narrow strip of Poly II to the shape shown. Be sure to cut the "waist" so that it is very narrow. Fold the section evenly at the waist and place in the wing former and burn away the excess.

2. The Poly II will melt together at the edges so it will be necessary to trim away the extreme edge so that the section will open up to the shape shown. Tie the formed wing into position with a series of figure eights. A drop of cement at the base, between the wings, will lock the wings in position permanently.

Poly-yarn Wing. Of all the upright-wing styles, this is the one that we use the most. In fact, we rarely bother with anything else anymore as this wing has all of the advantages going for it. It is quick and easy to tie, is extremely durable, and provides a good silhouette of the adult mayfly. Poly-yarn is available in all of the colors that are found in the wings of the mayflies. One of the best advantages is that the wing isn't cut to size until the winging operation is completed so that getting the right proportion is ensured.

1. Cut a section of poly-yarn and remove enough strands to get a bunch of the right size for the fly being tied (easy to do, since the yarn isn't twisted together). Hold the yarn across the hook shank, as shown, and anchor with two or three wraps of thread.

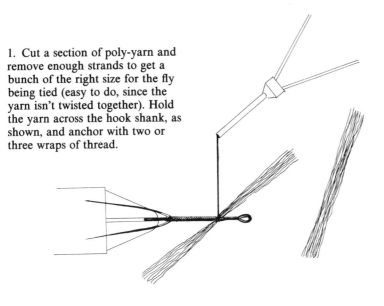

2. Pull the section back so that it is perpendicular to the hook and cross the thread in the other direction for two or three wraps.

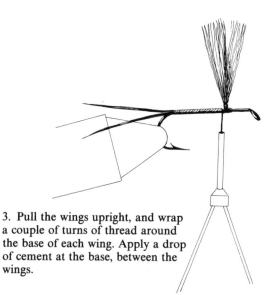

3. Pull the wings upright, and wrap a couple of turns of thread around the base of each wing. Apply a drop of cement at the base, between the wings.

Poly-wing Emerger. This type of wing is used to represent the emerging wing of the mayfly. Many times, the mature nymphs rise to the water's surface level, and an insect becomes trapped there by the surface tension as the nymphal shuck splits and the adult insect emerges. The wing is the first part of the adult to emerge from the nymphal case, and this wing is meant to represent that partially unfurled wing. It is an interesting question as to whether this is a nymph or a dry fly, but since we do want the imitation to float, we have included it with the dry-fly wings.

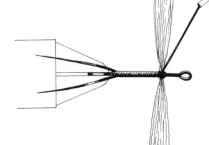

1. Tie in a section of poly-yarn at the forward end of the body.

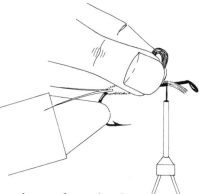

2. Fold the poly-yarn forward and tie down the end so that a small vertical loop is formed.

3. The finished wing. The dubbed body should now be completed around the wing.

There is, of course, another stage of the adult mayfly—the spinner. Flies tied to be representative of the spinner are tied with the wings in the "spent" position; the wings are positioned perpendicular to the body of the fly. If you will look back through the dry-fly wings that we have shown, you will readily see that most of the wing types can be easily tied spent by simply anchoring the wing in that position instead of the upright position.

STREAMER WINGS

Hair Wing. The hair wing is one of the most commonly called for type of wing on streamers. On most patterns, bucktail is the hair used, but some patterns utilize calf tail or squirrel. There are also streamer flies that use polar bear or black and brown bear. In short, any of the long hairs may be used.

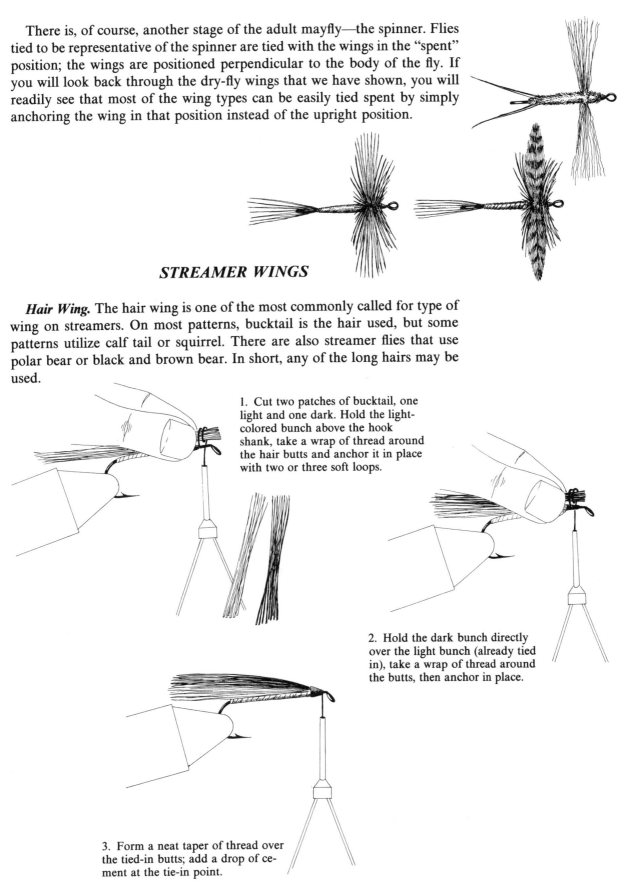

1. Cut two patches of bucktail, one light and one dark. Hold the light-colored bunch above the hook shank, take a wrap of thread around the hair butts and anchor it in place with two or three soft loops.

2. Hold the dark bunch directly over the light bunch (already tied in), take a wrap of thread around the butts, then anchor in place.

3. Form a neat taper of thread over the tied-in butts; add a drop of cement at the tie-in point.

Hackle-tip Wing. The hackle-tip wing provides a good body shape for the streamer, and if a good soft hackle is chosen, this wing type moves nicely in the water.

1. Select two hackles of the proper length and cut (don't tear) the fibres from the base of the hackle as shown.

2. Hold the hackles in place on the *top* of the hook and tie down using the soft loop. We left the short fibres on the butts to help anchor the hackles in place.

Marabou Wing. The marabou-wing streamer has been a favorite for many years and, no doubt, a great deal of its success can be attributed to the fact that marabou is so soft and moves, even appears to breathe, in the water. As with the hair-wing streamers, the marabou is usually tied with two colors of material: one light and one dark, with the dark section on top.

1. Cut a small patch of marabou from the feather stem. Marabou will be much easier to handle if it is kept wet during the whole tying process.

2. Hold the marabou in place and tie down, using two or three soft loops.

3. Tie in the second patch in the same manner. When the marabou dries, it will take on the full shape as shown.

Matuka-Style Wing. This is a really old technique of tying streamers that has really become popular again since it was brought to attention by Swisher and Richards, in their book, *Fly Fishing Strategy* (1975, Crown). The biggest advantage of this wing type is that it eliminates the problem of the hackle wing tangling around the bend of the hook. It also probably does a better job of simulating the tail movement of a minnow than the other winging methods.

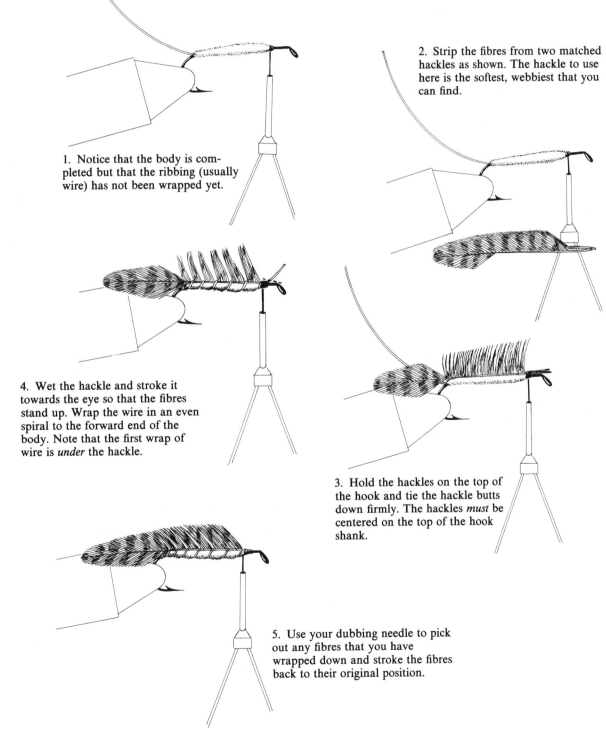

1. Notice that the body is completed but that the ribbing (usually wire) has not been wrapped yet.

2. Strip the fibres from two matched hackles as shown. The hackle to use here is the softest, webbiest that you can find.

3. Hold the hackles on the top of the hook and tie the hackle butts down firmly. The hackles *must* be centered on the top of the hook shank.

4. Wet the hackle and stroke it towards the eye so that the fibres stand up. Wrap the wire in an even spiral to the forward end of the body. Note that the first wrap of wire is *under* the hackle.

5. Use your dubbing needle to pick out any fibres that you have wrapped down and stroke the fibres back to their original position.

111

Quill Wing. There aren't many streamer patterns that call for this wing type but it is used on the Muddler Minnow and the popularity of that one pattern warrants the coverage of the winging method.

1. Cut two quill sections from a pair of matched turkey feathers (only one shown). Hold them in position on the top of the hook and anchor in position with two or three soft loops. The quill section will split very easily, so it is necessary to hold it *tightly* in position until it is firmly tied in.

2. Remember that once the wing is anchored, you cannot bring the thread back any farther on the wing or you will twist it out of shape.

Hopper-Style Wing. This isn't really a streamer wing, but the technique used is so similar to the quill wing that this seemed the most logical place to cover it.

1. Cut two matched quill sections. These sections must be mounted one at a time beginning with the far wing. The reason that they have to be tied in singly is because they are mounted on the side of the hook and you can't hold them in position and handle the soft loop at the same time.

2. The finished wing. Notice that the wings are mounted on the sides of the fly and that the tips of the quill sections are pointing *up*.

WING CASES

The mayflies and the stoneflies both undergo a complete metamorphosis, which means that they each have a true nymphal stage. During this stage, the developing wings are still inside the nymphal case and the area that they are under is covered by large platelike structures; this is what the fly tyer calls the wing case. In general appearance, the wing cases are well defined, and rather shiny. There are many methods of imitating the wing case and we are going to cover the most common.

Quill Wing Case. This is a very common method of tying a wing case and it is pretty fast and easy. Turkey has always been the material of choice because of the natural mottling of the feather, but goose, duck, or many other birds will work as well.

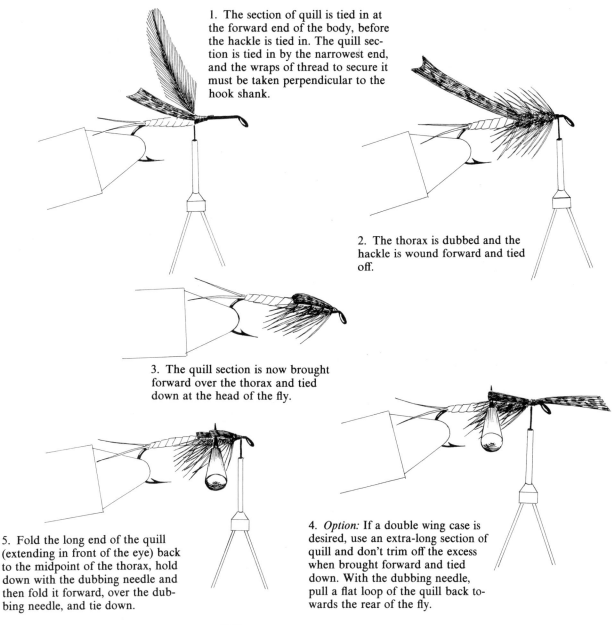

1. The section of quill is tied in at the forward end of the body, before the hackle is tied in. The quill section is tied in by the narrowest end, and the wraps of thread to secure it must be taken perpendicular to the hook shank.

2. The thorax is dubbed and the hackle is wound forward and tied off.

3. The quill section is now brought forward over the thorax and tied down at the head of the fly.

5. Fold the long end of the quill (extending in front of the eye) back to the midpoint of the thorax, hold down with the dubbing needle and then fold it forward, over the dubbing needle, and tie down.

4. *Option:* If a double wing case is desired, use an extra-long section of quill and don't trim off the excess when brought forward and tied down. With the dubbing needle, pull a flat loop of the quill back towards the rear of the fly.

Poly Wing Case. Poly-yarn is a good wing-case material as it is very easy to work with and gives a well-defined wing case that is very shiny.

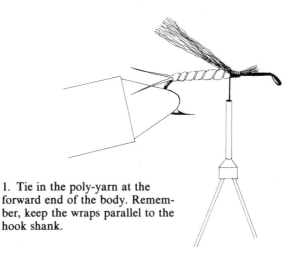

1. Tie in the poly-yarn at the forward end of the body. Remember, keep the wraps parallel to the hook shank.

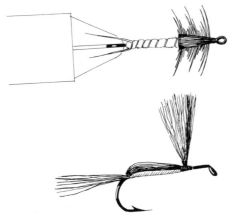

2. Form the thorax as desired and then fold the poly-yarn forward and tie off. The lower picture shows that a "poly-Humpy" can be tied in the same manner, with the poly-yarn also being used for the wing.

Hair Wing Case. The hair wing case is another method of achieving the definition and texture of the wing case found on nymphs. The method used is basically the same as for the poly-yarn wing case. The most important points concern the tying in of the hair for the wing case. Be sure that you bring the thread back far enough on the body so that there is no gap left there when the hair is folded forward, and be certain that you wrap the thread perpendicular to the hook shank so that there is a straight line formed across the back of the wing case when it is brought forward.

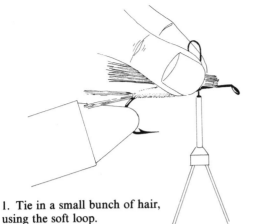

1. Tie in a small bunch of hair, using the soft loop.

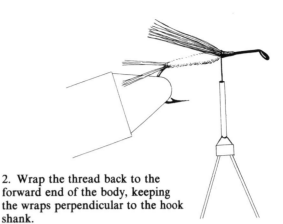

2. Wrap the thread back to the forward end of the body, keeping the wraps perpendicular to the hook shank.

3. Fold the bunch of hair forward over the completed thorax and tie down.

Cut or Burnt Feather Wing Case. The feather used for this wing case can be formed by either cutting the feather to shape or by using wing formers and burning it to shape. The wing former makes the job much easier and quicker, and ensures a symmetrical wing case.

1. Cut or burn the feather to shape and then tie it in just behind the eye of the hook. Note that the wing case extends past the forward end of the body.

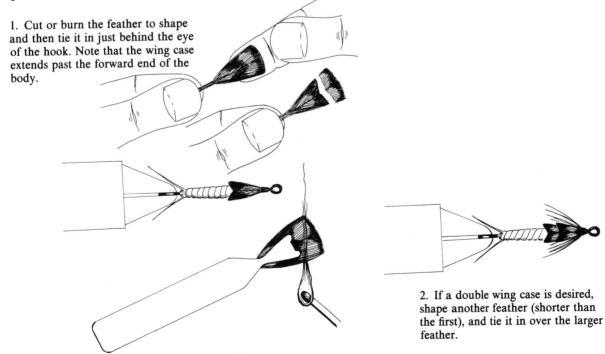

2. If a double wing case is desired, shape another feather (shorter than the first), and tie it in over the larger feather.

115

Poly II or Microweb Wing Case. These synthetic materials really make eye-catching wing cases. They have a texture that is very imitative of the wing cases on the natural insects and, of course, they are almost indestructible.

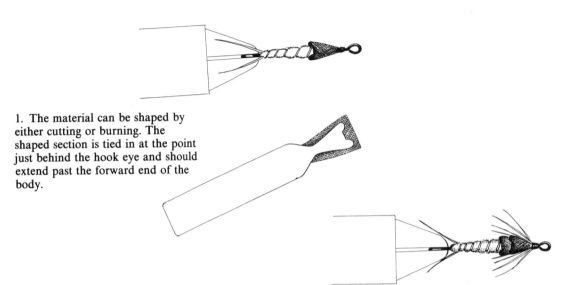

1. The material can be shaped by either cutting or burning. The shaped section is tied in at the point just behind the hook eye and should extend past the forward end of the body.

2. A shorter, second section can be added if you desire.

Latex Wing Case. Latex-sheet material (dental dam) makes a nice-looking wing case and has the advantage that you may color it as desired using permanent marking pens. Latex just won't work well in a wing former so you'll need to cut the sections to shape. The technique shown (doubling the material) is the best way to go about cutting any of the wing cases as it assures symmetry.

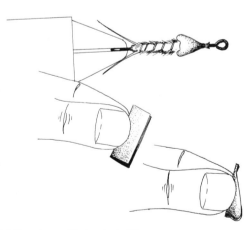

1. Fold the piece of latex in half lengthwise and, holding it firmly folded, cut one half of the shape. Unfold the section and tie it in just behind the eye of the hook.

2. Tie in a second, shorter section over the first. A drop of cement between the sections will help to anchor them in position.

eight
Hackle, Heads, and Legs

Nothing makes a fly appear amateurish as much as poorly handled hackle and/or a poorly finished head. Learning to handle hackle really is, at least partly, a matter of tying a lot of flies and developing a "feel" for working with the material. A nicely finished head, on the other hand, comes from simply taking the time to complete the head neatly before adding the whip finish and cutting the tying thread. It is a matter of *wanting* to get it right.

We're going to show you several different ways to add eyes to your flies, as seen on many streamers and the innovative, realistic flies that are so much a part of the recent fly-tying scene. If you've wondered how those neat little legs are tied on some of the nymphs, we're going to show you several ways to get the job done. Legs on flies are certainly questionable as far as being needed to catch fish, but they do make interesting flies and are just another adjunct to the fly tyer's repertoire that all finished tyers should possess.

HACKLE FOR NYMPHS AND WET FLIES

Throat Hackle. In some patterns, this is also called a beard. It is representative of the legs and unfurled wings on most patterns. The hackle chosen for the throat should be from a soft, webby feather and, quite often, body feathers from a grouse, one of the pheasants, or from a duck are used instead of neck hackle from a chicken.

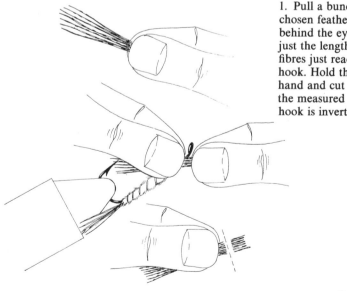

1. Pull a bunch of fibres from the chosen feather. Hold the feather just behind the eye of the hook and adjust the length so that the tips of the fibres just reach the point of the hook. Hold the fibres in the left hand and cut off the excess butts at the measured point. Note that the hook is inverted in the vise.

2. Hold the fibres in position and tie down firmly with a couple of soft loops.

117

3. The finished throat hackle. The tips of the throat hackle should just reach the point of the hook.

Throat Hackle (*variation*). This method of putting in the throat hackle is essentially the same as the one we just covered, but with an additional twist: The butts of the fibres are brought up to the top of the hook and tied in behind the head to establish the shape of a scud or, perhaps, to represent the emerging wing of a nymph.

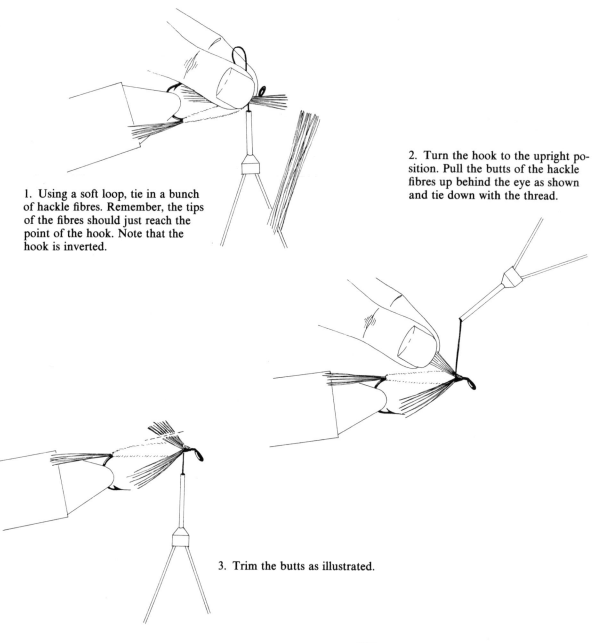

1. Using a soft loop, tie in a bunch of hackle fibres. Remember, the tips of the fibres should just reach the point of the hook. Note that the hook is inverted.

2. Turn the hook to the upright position. Pull the butts of the hackle fibres up behind the eye as shown and tie down with the thread.

3. Trim the butts as illustrated.

Throat Hackle (De Feo method). Here is a really simple, fast method of adding a throat hackle.

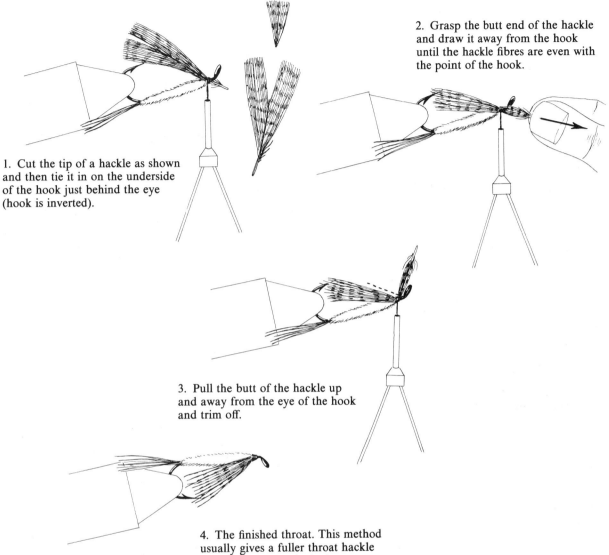

1. Cut the tip of a hackle as shown and then tie it in on the underside of the hook just behind the eye (hook is inverted).

2. Grasp the butt end of the hackle and draw it away from the hook until the hackle fibres are even with the point of the hook.

3. Pull the butt of the hackle up and away from the eye of the hook and trim off.

4. The finished throat. This method usually gives a fuller throat hackle than the other methods shown.

Collar Hackle. This is the most common type of hackle called for on the traditional wet flies. The composite illustration shows why you should discard the very butt end of the hackle stem and not attempt to use the full length of the hackle: Down at the butt of the hackle, the stem is usually oval in cross section, which causes the hackle to wrap on the hook across the narrowest dimension of the stem and flare the fibres along the hook shank instead of perpendicular to it. By discarding that butt and tying in farther up the stem, you reach the point where the stem is round in cross section and will wrap properly.

Another important point is the way the feather is tied in. For a wet-fly hackle, the feather is attached with the shiny side towards the tyer, so that when it is wrapped, the fibres will sweep towards the rear of the hook.

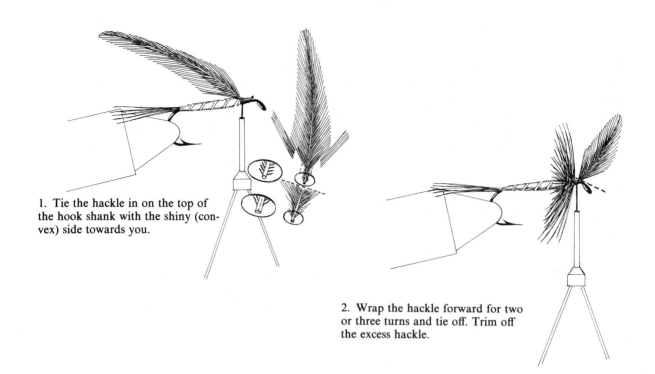

1. Tie the hackle in on the top of the hook shank with the shiny (convex) side towards you.

2. Wrap the hackle forward for two or three turns and tie off. Trim off the excess hackle.

Palmered Hackle. Palmering simply means that the hackle is wrapped in a spiral for the full length of the hook shank. Again, on a wet fly, we want the hackle fibres to bend back towards the bend of the hook, so it is necessary to tie in the hackle with the shiny side towards you.

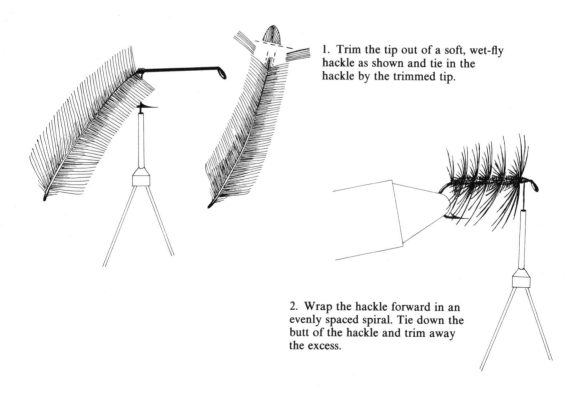

1. Trim the tip out of a soft, wet-fly hackle as shown and tie in the hackle by the trimmed tip.

2. Wrap the hackle forward in an evenly spaced spiral. Tie down the butt of the hackle and trim away the excess.

DRY-FLY HACKLE

The biggest difference between wet-fly and dry-fly hackle is, of course, the hackle used. Dry-fly hackle must be very stiff so that it can support the fly on the water's surface. Although this is the biggest difference, there are some additional points to be considered. One of these is that we tie a dry fly hackle in so that the dull side (convex) is facing us. This way, the fibres will flare forward towards the eye of the hook and better resist the bending action of the fibres as the fly is brought through the water at the completion of most drifts.

Fore-and-Aft Hackle. The fore-and-aft hackles on a dry fly serve a very important function, particularly the addition of the aft hackle. The bend area of a hook is the heaviest part and a fly tied with an aft hackle has the additional support of a hackle at that point.

1. Tie the hackle in at the bend with the dull side facing you. Advance the tying thread so that you have room to wrap the hackle.

2. Wind three or four turns of hackle and tie off the tip.

3. Shape the desired body and tie in another hackle at the forward end.

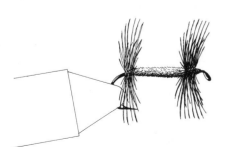

4. Wrap the hackle three or four turns forward, tie off, and trim away the excess tip.

Palmered Hackle. The technique here is the same as used for the palmered wet fly except that the hackle is tied in with the dull side towards you.

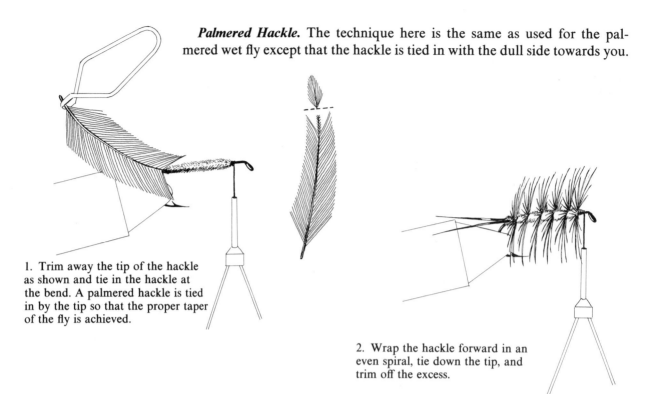

1. Trim away the tip of the hackle as shown and tie in the hackle at the bend. A palmered hackle is tied in by the tip so that the proper taper of the fly is achieved.

2. Wrap the hackle forward in an even spiral, tie down the tip, and trim off the excess.

Standard Dry-fly Hackle. This is the most common method of hackling a dry fly and is used on the vast majority of patterns. Notice, in particular, how the hackle stem is tied in: The stem is bound down behind the wing and then again in front of the wing; this ensures that the hackle won't pull out when you start winding it.

1. Strip the fibres from near the butt of the hackle and tie it in behind the wing (dull side facing you), bring the thread ahead of the wing and bind down the stem again.

2. Take the first couple of turns of hackle behind the wing. Tipping the wing slightly forward will give you more room and also allow you to get the last wrap closer to the wing.

122

3. Bring the hackle under the wing and continue wrapping forward. Tip the wing back slightly so that the first wrap in front of it is against the wing.

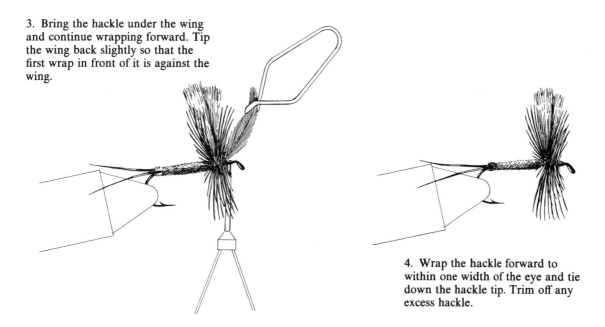

4. Wrap the hackle forward to within one width of the eye and tie down the hackle tip. Trim off any excess hackle.

Double Hackle. A double hackle on a fly doesn't really add much to the support provided because there is only so much room for hackle on a fly and a single hackle will fill that area. The reason that a double hackle is used is to get a color mix. There is a slight amount of support gained because the two hackles are tied in facing opposite directions so that the fibres of one flare forward and the fibres of the other flare back, but there probably isn't much of a real gain.

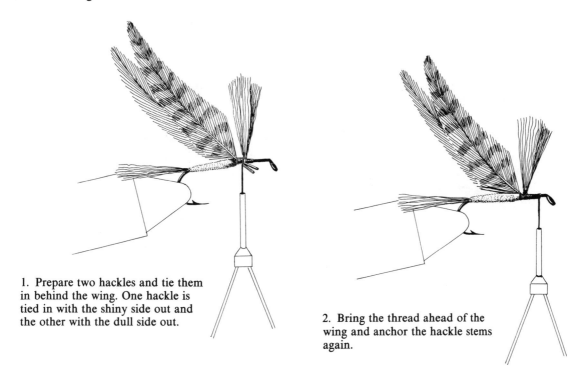

1. Prepare two hackles and tie them in behind the wing. One hackle is tied in with the shiny side out and the other with the dull side out.

2. Bring the thread ahead of the wing and anchor the hackle stems again.

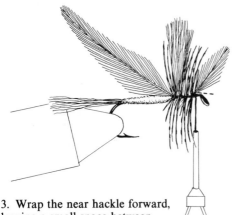

3. Wrap the near hackle forward, leaving a small space between wraps. Tie down the tip and trim away the excess.

4. Wrap the second hackle forward, spacing it between the turns of the first hackle. Tie down and trim off the tip.

Double Hackle (*Streamer*). Wrapping two hackles at a time is possible, *if* the hackles are long enough to be held and wrapped with the fingers. This is usually not the case when hackling a dry fly, but on streamers, the hackle (often saddle hackle) may be long enough to handle this way. The reason that you can't wrap two hackles at a time with hackle pliers is that the diameter of the stems of the two hackles are almost certain to be of different sizes. This means that one of the hackles will shorten up faster than the other as they are wound. By holding the hackle in your fingers, you can allow one hackle to slip as they are wound, while still keeping tension on both.

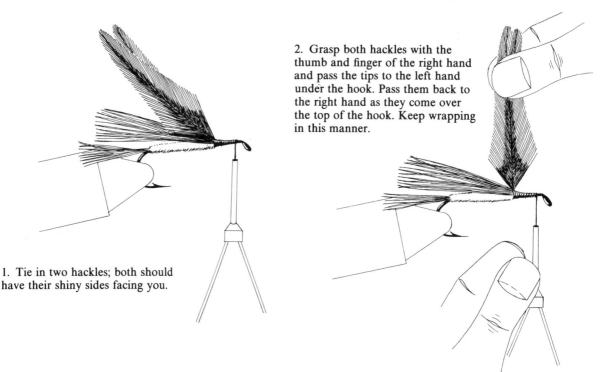

2. Grasp both hackles with the thumb and finger of the right hand and pass the tips to the left hand under the hook. Pass them back to the right hand as they come over the top of the hook. Keep wrapping in this manner.

1. Tie in two hackles; both should have their shiny sides facing you.

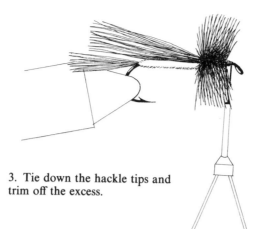

3. Tie down the hackle tips and trim off the excess.

Parachute Hackle. There are several methods of tying a parachute hackle, and you can even buy a tool (called a gallows tool) to assist with the operation. There are times when parachute-hackled flies seem to work better than conventionally hackled flies. There may be a number of reasons for this: The hackle actually acts like a parachute allowing the angler to make a really delicate presentation, and a fly tied with a parachute hackle sits much lower in the water, which seems to appeal to the trout at times. The method we show is used on a fly with a single, upright hair wing.

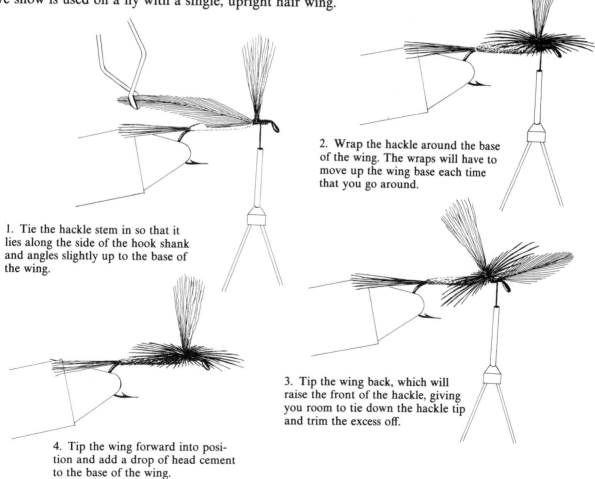

1. Tie the hackle stem in so that it lies along the side of the hook shank and angles slightly up to the base of the wing.

2. Wrap the hackle around the base of the wing. The wraps will have to move up the wing base each time that you go around.

3. Tip the wing back, which will raise the front of the hackle, giving you room to tie down the hackle tip and trim the excess off.

4. Tip the wing forward into position and add a drop of head cement to the base of the wing.

LEGS

There are many different ways of simulating the legs of a fly, and the ones that we show here are really just representative of the techniques used. The actual *need* for legs on a fly is questionable, but there are a number of patterns tied with legs and, besides, they are challenging and fun to tie.

Cut-feather Legs. This method of tying legs on a nymph has been around for a long time and, although not the most realistic, it does produce some pretty good-looking legs that move and provide some animation.

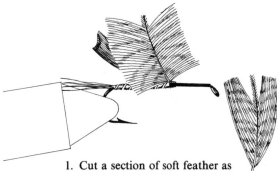

1. Cut a section of soft feather as shown; the length of the feathered section should be equal to the thorax area of the fly. Tie the prepared feather in at the forward end of the body.

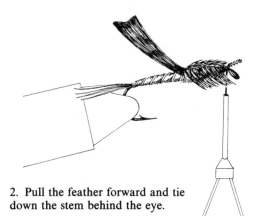

2. Pull the feather forward and tie down the stem behind the eye.

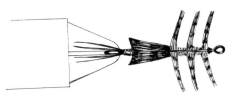

3. Cut out sections of fibres in the pattern shown.

4. Coat the remaining bunches of fibres with cement and pinch them together by sliding them between your fingers. In this example, the thorax would then be dubbed and the wing case brought forward to complete the fly.

Monofilament Legs. This is a cute trick, and one that is easy to pull off. You use ordinary monofilament fishing line and color it with permanent marking pens to get the desired color.

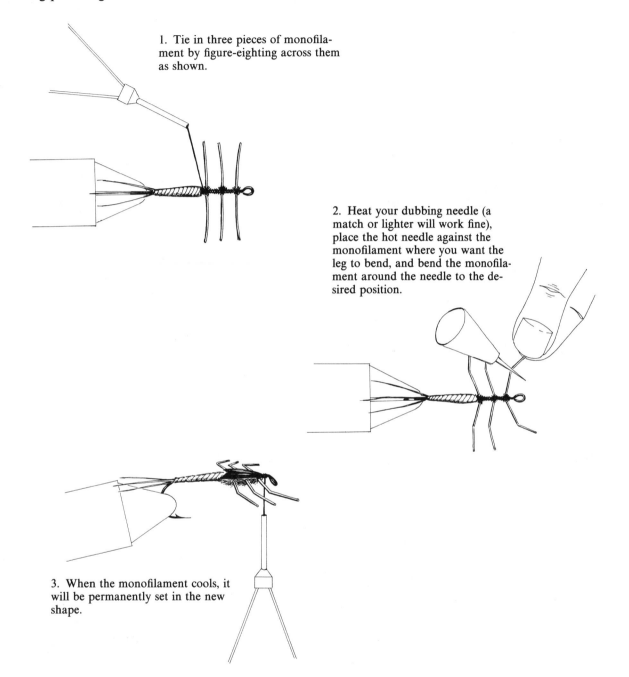

1. Tie in three pieces of monofilament by figure-eighting across them as shown.

2. Heat your dubbing needle (a match or lighter will work fine), place the hot needle against the monofilament where you want the leg to bend, and bend the monofilament around the needle to the desired position.

3. When the monofilament cools, it will be permanently set in the new shape.

Hackle Legs. This is another interesting method for tying those realistic legs you see on the super-detailed nymphs. As with most of the flimsy appendages in this section, these won't stand up very well and are really better suited for looking at than using, but, nonetheless, it is an interesting technique. The illustration is pretty self-explanatory, but we'll run through the steps from top to bottom in the picture.

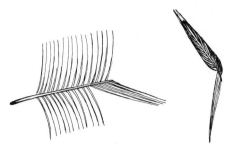

1. Flare the fibres of a hackle so that they stand out perpendicular to the hackle stem.

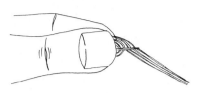

2. Fold the fibres of one entire side and the majority of the other side in reverse to their normal position.

3. Apply head cement to the hackle and allow it to dry; then add another coat of cement to the prepared feather.

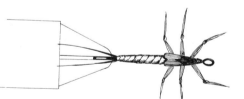

4. Tie in six of these formed legs in pairs as shown on the completed fly.

Knotted Legs and Hopper Legs. This time we'll let the pictures do the talking. The first illustration shows the method used to tie the legs and the second shows them in use. You will need to cement the legs in both cases.

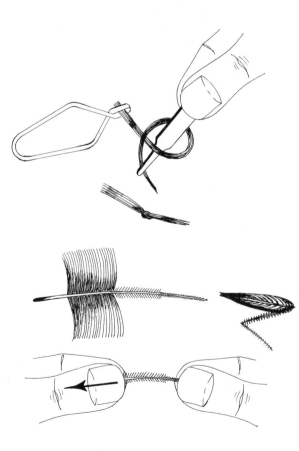

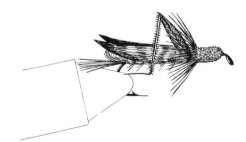

HEADS, EYES, AND ANTENNAE

Here are a few miscellaneous tying techniques to really put the finishing touches on some of your flies.

Spun-hair Head. The Muddler Minnow is probably the fly that first comes to mind when you think of a spun-hair head, but the technique is also used on some other flies. It is a good head for grasshoppers because it will provide the bulk needed so that you can shape the head to establish the blocky form of the grasshopper. The method used is really the same that we showed in the section on bodies with just a few minor differences.

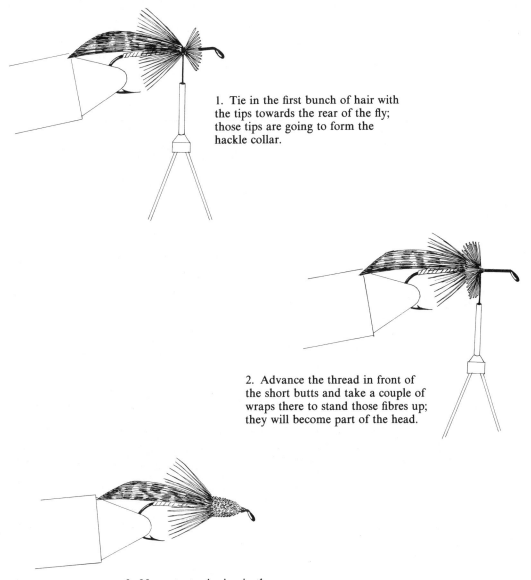

1. Tie in the first bunch of hair with the tips towards the rear of the fly; those tips are going to form the hackle collar.

2. Advance the thread in front of the short butts and take a couple of wraps there to stand those fibres up; they will become part of the head.

3. Now, start spinning in the patches of hair just as before, trim to the rough shape, and then singe to finish the head.

Reversed-hair Head. This is a good substitute for the spun-hair head and is much quicker and easier to tie.

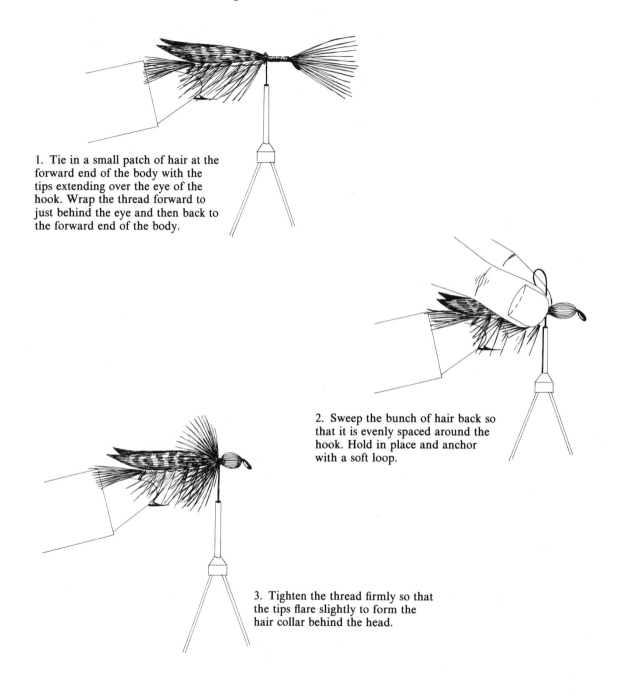

1. Tie in a small patch of hair at the forward end of the body with the tips extending over the eye of the hook. Wrap the thread forward to just behind the eye and then back to the forward end of the body.

2. Sweep the bunch of hair back so that it is evenly spaced around the hook. Hold in place and anchor with a soft loop.

3. Tighten the thread firmly so that the tips flare slightly to form the hair collar behind the head.

Monofilament Eyes. I wondered for years how in the world tyers got those good-looking, round little eyes on their flies. I thought they were tying in some sort of a little ball and tried using the heads of map tacks to achieve the result ... they looked pretty good but kept falling out. Here's how it's done!

1. Tie a short piece of monofilament fishing line across the hook shank as shown. Use figure eights to anchor it in place.

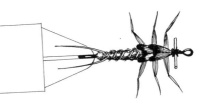

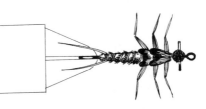

2. Continue figure-eighting the thread until a nice head shape is formed.

3. Use the bottom edge of a match flame, or a cigarette, to melt the end of the monofilament. It's magic, a perfect round eyeball appears!

Painted Eyes. This is nothing new but is one of those things that you might never think of unless someone shows you, and it is so simple. Streamers are the primary users of painted eyes but there is no reason not to use the technique on other styles of flies as well.

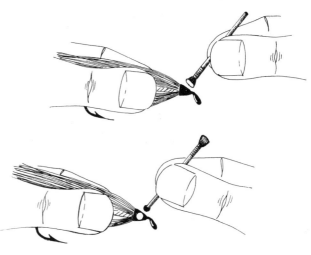

1. Put a coat of head cement on the finished head and when it is tacky, add a drop of white paint, using the large end of a finishing nail. When the white paint is tacky, add a drop of black paint, using the small end of the nail (file the end flat).

In many cases, the antennae, when used on a fly, are just tails added at the head end of the imitation. Usually the antenna serves only to represent the same body part as on the natural insect; however, there are a few cases where the antennae serve a purpose and our first type of antennae is one of these.

Hackle Stem Antennae. This style of antennae is used on a pattern called the Goddard Caddis, which was first tied to be used on lakes imitating the skittering or fluttering caddis. Because the fly was meant to be moved over the surface of the water by the angler, the long, firm antennae were needed to keep the fly from tipping forward and drowning by the movement. It is a good technique any time that long antennae are desired.

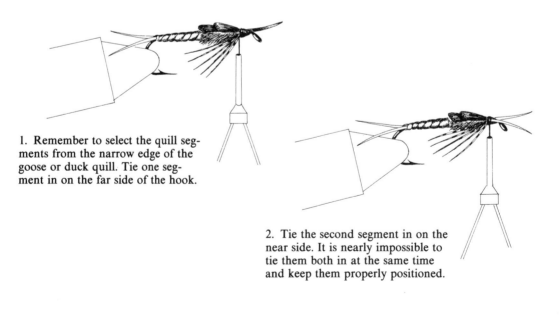

1. Strip the fibres from two matched hackles and tie one in on each side of the head of the fly.

2. By stroking the hackle stems between the fingernails, as shown, a curve can be formed.

Quill Antennae. As illustrated, the quill antennae are tied in the same manner as the quill tails that we discussed earlier.

1. Remember to select the quill segments from the narrow edge of the goose or duck quill. Tie one segment in on the far side of the hook.

2. Tie the second segment in on the near side. It is nearly impossible to tie them both in at the same time and keep them properly positioned.

Hair Antennae. Again, the antennae are tied just as the tail, and on the illustrated fly, it is really apparent since they are both tied in before the body or wing of the fly is tied.

1. After tying in the two bunches of hair for the tail, repeat the process just behind the eye of the hook. Form whatever type of body is desired.

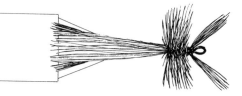

2. Add the wing and the hackle and then lacquer or wax the tail and antennae patches so they will hold their shape.

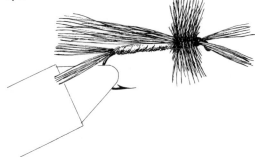

nine
Judging Quality

In order to judge your own flies, it is necessary that you understand just what points separate the really good, properly tied fly from those that are just adequate. As we will see, there are many things that affect the overall appearance of the finished fly but, by far, the most important thing is proportion.

Proportion

If there is one point that immediately identifies a high-quality fly, it is proportion! The materials used, symmetry, neatness, practicality, consistency, and all the other attributes that we strive for are really for naught if the fly's parts are not in proportion to each other.

The essentials of proportion are relatively simple. The tail should be equal to the distance from the back of the eye to the start of the bend on wets and nymphs, and equal to the distance from the front of the eye to the start of the bend on dries. The body should begin at a point directly opposite the point of the barb and end halfway between the point of the hook and the back of the eye. The hackle should be 1½ times the gap of the hook, and the wings should be twice the gap. The head should be equal to the size of the eye.

That makes it all very cut and dried *except*—those proportions will only work if you are tying on a round-bend hook. A tail length equal to the distance from the back of the eye to the start of the bend is going to be a mite short if you are tying on a limerick hook because the bend starts much closer to the eye than on a round-bend hook of the same size.

You should find yourself adjusting the proportions on some of your patterns as you tie them. If you want your caddis larva imitation to have more of a curved shape to its body, you may decide to start the body farther back on the hook, down in the bend area. If the fly is tied well, though, it will still appear to be in proportion because the adjustment you have made is natural looking for that given pattern.

Another reason for changing proportion slightly is to increase or decrease the size of the fly slightly to better imitate a particular insect. When tying for really close imitation of an insect you may find the natural's size is actually between hook sizes: smaller than a normally tied #16, but larger than a normally tied #18. It's a pretty easy matter to tie a "#17" on either a #16 or a #18 hook by simply adjusting the size of the body parts while keeping them in proportion to one another.

At a recent outdoor show, a very enthusiastic, knowledgeable young man came to the booth to chat and was adamant in his need for odd-numbered hooks so that he could tie these in-between sized imitations. He just wouldn't agree that the tyer should be able to make that much adjustment in fly size. His argument was that if you tied a "#17" imitation on a number 16 or 18 hook, then the fly was out of proportion and, therefore, not tied properly.

First of all, he had lost track of the reason for tying flies—to catch fish. If that #17 imitation is really needed to fool the trout, who cares if the fly's proportion isn't exactly by the "rules"? Secondly, the difference in total length (back of bend to front of eye) between a #16 and an #18 dry-fly hook is about 1/16th of an inch; to tie a number 17 would mean, at most, a 1/32nd of an inch adjustment in total length or about 1/12th of the fly's length.

Proper proportion really isn't as easy to define as any of us would like. We use the rules that were first outlined because we need to give the beginner some criteria for judgment. You shouldn't become too tied to them, however. Once you have advanced beyond the basics you should develop an almost instinctive feel for proper sizing of fly parts and this feel is what you use to judge if the fly is correct in proportion.

Neatness

We have taught some tyers who were able to pick up all the techniques needed to tie virtually any fly, developed their feel for proportion to a fine degree, were innovative, really had perfected all of the skills of the good fly tyer who will never tie good-looking flies for the lack of neatness. You've seen it too (hopefully not in *your* flies); that little space between the end of the body and the start of the wing case, the misshapen head, unevenly spaced ribbing, or the tipped-down tail. Any one of these will make the otherwise great fly look shoddy.

For most people, all that is needed is to point out these flaws, and that particular mistake isn't made again. After a couple of corrections, they start understanding what types of things are important and begin correcting them on their own. But, in our experience, the individual who doesn't pick up quickly on these points will tie untidy flies forever. It probably isn't even too much of a serious flaw as far as the fish-taking ability of the fly is concerned, and usually the individual isn't even aware of the problem, but you can bet that every other fly tyer will cast a jaded glance at those flies.

Symmetry

A lack of symmetry is an often unnoticed flaw in a fly. The fly may be judged as just not being neat or properly proportioned when the real problem is that the fly isn't symmetrical.

Probably the most common example of this is a dry fly whose wings aren't mounted so that each extends out from the body at the same angle from vertical. Other common problems are bodies that are lopsided, heads that are misshapen, forked tails that are of different lengths or project at different angles from the rear of the body, and a myriad other instances where two like parts of the fly aren't mirror images of one another.

The lack of symmetry may not only be an annoying error to the eye, it tends to unbalance a fly. A dry fly whose wings aren't symmetrical will tend to whirl when cast, leading to a twisted leader and wind knots. A streamer that has a lopsided body will not move in the water like a real minnow. In short, nature is always symmetrical and when our fly isn't, some of the naturalness that we are striving for is lost.

Practicality

All of us who have tied for some period of time have gotten caught on this one. Several years ago, I developed an outstanding caddis dry fly. It used a mallard body feather that had the fibres reversed for the wing. As the fibres were reversed, the feather assumed a perfect caddis shape. When observed from underneath, the texture of the wing was very imitative. The owner of the store I was tying for at the time was as enthusiastic as I was over the pattern and ordered several dozen in assorted colors and sizes. They were immediate successes because they caught the fishermen's eye. The first report we got on them was that they were also very successful on the stream. I couldn't have been more pleased and, I must admit, was just a little impressed with my genius. Then the other reports started coming it—they really did take fish—one fish per fly! Every time that a fish took the fly, the beautiful wing was shredded, rendering the fly unusable. We quickly dropped that pattern from the line; it just wasn't practical.

Along the same line, I often look at some of the hyper-realistic patterns that are displayed in magazines from time to time and even tie some of those I find interesting. I enjoy them for their beauty, and for the challenge that they present, but I can't help but question the practicality of using a fly that took a couple of hours to assemble.

Another example of the impractical fly is the one that requires really rare (sometimes one-of-a kind) materials. There isn't a whole lot to be said for spending time developing a new pattern that requires some material that you only have a very limited quantity of and can't replenish. We've all seen this carried a step further by the innovator then publishing the pattern so that we all can drive the fly-department shop proprietors insane by asking for "rhesus monkey belly hair" or whatever. Again, the fly may be efficient but it just isn't practical.

Quality of Materials

This area seems so blatantly obvious that it isn't worth commenting on, but, unfortunately it is one of the common problems seen, particularly in the commercial market. Dry flies tied with hackle that wouldn't do a bass bug justice, poorly dyed materials that blanch back to the original color when put in the water, poor quality hooks (this is very common)—the hook is the most expensive part of the fly and the tyer can really save money here—are all examples of the problem.

One of the roots of the problem is that when we teach the beginner we usually recommend that he use something less than top-quality materials since the finished product won't be good enough to warrant using the "good stuff." There are two fallacies here. First of all, you are implying that you expect something other than a good finished product and, more than likely, that's what you will get! Secondly, the cost difference between tying with top-quality materials and "acceptable" materials is pennies per fly. Is that worth cheating your student or yourself out of the pleasures of working with superior materials? Besides, if the fly does turn out to be of good quality, and you've embellished it with poor materials, it just isn't worth the few pennies, is it?

Consistency

You will often hear it said about a commercial tyer, "He's really good, every fly that he ties looks just like every other fly that he ties." And it's true, the really good commercial tyer will turn out a dozen flies and you can't tell number six from the first or last one but this shouldn't be a criterion applied only to the guy or gal who is tying commercially.

Tying with consistency means that you won't tie up a half-dozen of a pattern and then only use four of them on the stream because the other two aren't quite good enough. Most of us don't have unlimited time to spend at the tying bench, certainly not enough that we can afford to tie flies that we can't or won't use. By being more consistent we can use the hour at the bench more efficiently without any loss of the pleasure to be had there. In fact, if you need to get out a half-dozen Adams for tomorrow's trip and you only have to tie six flies instead of eight or ten to get the six you need, you might have time to tie the new pattern you've been wanting to try.

The reason that the commercial tyer is consistent is because he or she ties with a lot of repetition. When you set down to tie an order for thirty dozen of a pattern you will be consistent after about the first two dozen and that's the key to the amateur tyer developing consistency: When you tie a pattern, tie several of the same pattern before changing to something else. Not only will your flies start looking better and better, your fly boxes will always be full of usable flies.

All quality flies share the attributes of proper proportion, neatness, symmetry, quality materials, practicality, and consistency. These, then, are the attributes that you should use when judging *your* flies.

ten

Beyond the Amateur

Virtually without exception, every single one of you is going to become a "professional" fly tyer! According to Webster, one of the definitions of professional is: "participating for gain or livelihood in an activity or field of endeavor often engaged in by amateurs." Obviously, if you start tying flies commercially you are performing as a professional, but what if you trade a few dozen flies to your buddy for that rod of his that you have coveted for so long? Aren't you "participating for gain"? If the local TU pays you a few bucks to teach a tying class for some of their members, aren't you performing as a professional? You bet you are, and virtually every fly tyer is going to fall into one of these categories sooner or later.

As subtly hinted at above, there are two facets of professional fly-tying: tying flies for sale (or trade) and teaching. Each of these approaches into professionalism has its difficulties and problems as well as certain rewards.

Tying flies for resale is tried, at one time or another, by just about every fly tyer. If you enjoy tying, why not get paid for it, seems to be the reasoning, and it is a rational way of looking at it. If you want to give it a try, we can almost guarantee that your first visit to a fly shop will result in a sale! There just aren't enough commercial tyers available to keep all the fly boxes in the shops around the country full. That should give you a hint that there's a hitch in the process somewhere. Well, really there are several.

You probably have a pretty complete selection of hooks lying around . . . most of a box of all the popular styles in the common sizes, right? When you get that first order for 10 dozen of one pattern, in one size, it probably won't even dawn on you that you need more than a full box just for this order. There isn't a chance that you have a neck that will tie ten dozen flies of one size. Have you got extra thread? It will take nearly a full spool just for these ten dozen. The logistics get the beginning commercial tyer every time! I well remember my first foray into the ranks of the professional.

I approached the store for the most valid of reasons—I needed to make some extra money. The shop owner was most friendly (almost gleeful, in retrospect), he explained to me that he had tyers who provided him with the bulk of his needs, one tied nothing but nymphs and streamers, and another tied all of the dries, what he needed was someone to tie all of the "odd" stuff. He needed me to tie the small quantity patterns that just weren't big sellers since the two pros he had wouldn't bother with "small" orders. Sounded great to me!

Then he started through the fly boxes, ordering three dozen of this in three different sizes, six dozen of that, another five dozen of these, some dark and some light, and so on. When he had finished I had an order for 38 dozen flies. I made a quick observation that I had everything that I needed

138

except some light deer hair (which I bought) and exuberantly set out for home and the tying bench.

Thirty-eight dozen flies is 456 of the little rascals and a disproportionate number of them were *little* rascals. After tying about four-dozen #18 Irresistibles, I began to wonder if anyone had ever tied them for him, much less in the past year. A lot of the order was in really small quantities; a dozen of each of five different sizes, two dozen of one pattern, and it seemed to me that the guy who was tying the dry flies must really be falling behind because that's about all that was in my order.

Well, I ended up making four trips back to the shop to replenish materials which the owner graciously put on my tab against the order. I filled *my* fly boxes with the flies I tied that I felt really weren't good enough for sale. I was up until midnight virtually every night (in my supreme confidence I had promised delivery in a week). I made it, though, and I was really proud when I hauled those flies in to the shop to collect my money.

The surprises weren't over yet, however! I only got about half the money I had figured on because of the materials I had charged against the order. He had already compiled a list of another 55 dozen that he needed (said that he didn't want to overload me on the first order). Being a little wiser this time, I made a closer inspection of quantities, as well as type, of materials that I needed—and went home broke. Needless to say, my wife was very impressed with my new job!

I went to work in that store after tying for them for a couple of years and saw the drama unfold time and time again. We never could keep the fly boxes full of the odd patterns and there was a never-ending stream of tyers who took on the job. Some of them did deliver one order. I don't think anyone but me ever stuck with it beyond one shot. (I really did need the money.) Several of them took the order with enthusiasm and were never seen again. The reasons are many.

The average, avid fly tyer may tie fifteen or twenty dozen flies a year and just has no concept of how large a quantity forty or fifty dozen flies really is—especially when they have to be done in a week or two. The new guy or gal is always going to get stuck with the patterns that none of the regular tyers want to bother with; the ones that are slow to tie, or are only needed in small quantities, or that require expensive materials.

To the commercial tyer, time is money and those slow patterns quickly cut into the hourly wage earned at the vise. Small quantities also eat into the profit because of the time needed to get set up to tie a particular pattern. Since most commercial tyers furnish their own materials, that, too, cuts the profit.

By the end of the first season, I was delivering the flies that I tied directly into the stock boxes and looking through the boxes and taking the next order on my own. I worked in the store for four years and we never, ever had any #18 Irresistibles after the batch I tied were gone. Somehow my eye just never seemed to catch the fact that we were out and my successors were, apparently, smarter than me from the outset.

There are, however, some points to be considered. First of all, I did make good money. When you are tying in large quantities, you develop some pretty sophisticated techniques to speed up the process and all that practice also increases your speed. Because I was reliable and did deliver my orders on time, I was soon able to be a bit more selective on what I tied, and I left behind for the next new tyer the really miserable stuff.

But what was more important to me, I became a fly tyer! We've talked with a lot of other instructors and professional tyers about the learning process and most seem to agree that it takes about a hundred dozen flies through the vise before most people really start becoming "expert" fly tyers. When you are tying commercially, that hundred dozen comes pretty darn quick.

Finally, as a commercial tyer you are accepted. Other professional tyers start paying attention to what you are doing and start sharing their techniques, methods, and sources of supplies with you. I've even seen tyers team up on a big order for Irresistibles with one tyer mounting the tail and doing all of the hair spinning and the other mounting the wings and hackling the fly. Professional tyers are an elite group because it takes a special kind of person to sit hour after hour tying the same fly without ending up in the "funny farm."

We think every fly tyer should have at least one try at tying commercially just for the experience. You can't help but become a better tyer much faster than by tying flies only for your own needs. If tying professionally suits your talent and personality, there is good money to be made. If it doesn't really suit you, you can't appreciate how great the pleasure is when you quit and can sit at the bench and tie whatever you want, as slowly as you want, without feeling guilty about "wasting" the time!

There's another point about commercial tying and, in particular, about the commercial fly tyer. The pro tyers are often *not* the best tyers around. Because he or she is tying for money, the commercial tyer often tries to tie as few different styles of flies as possible. Don't misunderstand; most commercial tyers can tie just about anything, but they just won't spend the time to experiment with new patterns, to tie the super-realistic flies, or to learn how to tie the old salmon flies. They certainly could do it if they would spend the time (pick it up pretty fast, too) but every hour that they spend tying for their own enjoyment is money not earned. The real top-quality tyers are mostly amateurs and/or fly-tying instructors.

The fly-tying instructor represents the other aspect of the professional fly tyer and, as difficult as it is for the shop owner to find enough commercial tyers, it is probably more difficult to find a *good* fly-tying instructor. Finding a good tyer who is willing to teach is not the problem. The problem is finding a good tyer who *can* teach. Teaching of any sort requires a special talent; we've all been exposed to teachers who had full command of their material but just couldn't relate the material to the class. This is the most often-seen problem for the tying instructor.

In order to teach fly-tying, the instructor must be a good fly tyer and that is often the problem: The tying instructor must be able to "teach down" to his students without "talking down" to them. First of all, it is very easy to teach over the students' heads because the teacher is so accustomed to the tying steps that he isn't even aware of the details of the steps he performs. It is a real battle for the instructor to recall just how difficult it was to get the thread started on the hook the first time he tried it.

Secondly, it is very easy for the instructor to become bored with teaching material that is far below his own level of expertise. Tying really basic flies isn't very challenging or interesting to the individual who has been tying for years and, perhaps, gets his enjoyment from tying detailed salmon flies. Yes, it takes a very special person to be a good tying instructor.

There are certain personality traits that are an inherent part of the makeup of any good teacher: Patience, open-mindedness, friendliness, genuine interest in material being taught and, perhaps more importantly, a genuine interest in the student, are all needed if the instructor is to be effective. It is, of course, important that the tying instructor is a competent fly tyer and knowledgeable in related areas such as basic aquatic entomology, but it is more important that he have the needed attributes of an instructor.

Just as the instructor must be possessed of certain traits, there is also the need for some knowledge in the area of teaching methods. Most tying instructors just seem to teach "off the top of their heads," which results in a rather disorganized presentation. No professional teacher would consider approaching an upcoming class without the preparation of, at least, a lesson outline and most would probably prefer to teach from a complete lesson plan.

By preparing the lesson plan, the teacher accomplishes several goals at once: The relationship of one part of the material to another, separating the really important items from those which aren't as necessary, reviewing the subject matter, being certain that all needed materials are available, presenting the correct amount of material, and being sure that the desired learning outcomes of the lesson are met. All these fall neatly into focus as the lesson plan is developed on paper. With these items taken care of before class time, the instructor is then ready to devote all of his effort to the "fun" part of teaching, the presentation.

The presentation of the course material should be natural and enjoyable. The teaching of a fly-tying class is almost a tutorial type of instruction. Although there are several students present, much of your time will be spent working with one student at a time. Most instructors demonstrate the particular steps or a particular pattern to the group and then as the students begin accomplishing the steps, the instructor roams among them, offering assistance here and there as needed on an individual basis. This allows the instructor to get to know the weaknesses and strengths of each student as well as developing a particular teaching approach that is effective when dealing with each individual.

Teaching a tying class really isn't difficult if you take the time to adequately prepare the lesson material in advance, but there are a few stumbling blocks. It seems that in every class there is the student who has tied before and is certain to let you and the rest of the class know it! The problem you'll have with this student is getting him to pay attention. While you are demonstrating or explaining something he will be mentally (on occasion, audibly) comparing what you are saying or doing to what he already knows about it and when you are done, he doesn't really remember what *you* said. The best way to deal with this individual is to ask him questions as you go along. Since he was sure to let the whole class know that he already knew something about the material, he won't want to be caught unable to answer the question and will start being more attentive to what you are teaching.

Probably the most difficult student to deal with is the "passive learner."

He paid his money for you to teach him to tie flies and doesn't feel that he should have to exert any effort to get his money's worth. His efforts at tying are limited to a quick, half-hearted attempt at each pattern, and, yet, he is not too happy that his flies aren't as good as the others in the class. I guess we're supposed to unscrew the top of his head and pour the talent in! There is a way, however, to deal with the problem. You will probably have at least one youngster in the class; ask our lackadaisical friend to "help" the kid along. I'll guarantee that the youngster is paying close attention to your instruction and is tying better than the disinterested party. No adult is going to allow himself to be outshone by a young boy or girl, especially when there are other adults around, and he is supposed to be helping the youngster.

The opposite of this is the father (mother) who is enrolled in the class with his (her) son or daughter and insists on interpreting all of your instruction for the child. The child quickly becomes confused with the two sets of instructions, and then the parents become upset that the youngster isn't doing too well, and, after all, how does that make *them* look to the class? The solution to this is to ask the youngster to move down closer to you (away from the parent, really) so that you can be sure that he or she can see and hear. I guarantee that after two patterns away from mom or dad, the kid will be tying better than the parent.

There are several other types of individuals who seem to show up in class just to make your life difficult, but we would take some of the challenge and fun out of the teaching experience if we listed them all and, besides, we have taught enough to know that we haven't seen them all yet. There is one group, however, that is a real joy to work with—the youngsters!

Kids are still used to learning, they're in school every day and don't have any hang-ups about listening and watching you teach, especially something as much fun as fly-tying. They just naturally accept that you are the world's greatest tyer and that anything you say is gospel. They really want to please you and never try to impress you with their own knowledge. Best of all, they are completely natural and spontaneous. My oldest son went through one of Don's classes when he was seven years old. The first night of class, the fellow sitting next to him was attempting to impress the class by expounding, at great length, on the horrors of someone using live bait in the pursuit of trout. When Mace asked him, in childish innocence, why he didn't kill it before he used it if it bothered him so much, everyone roared, and the class started to become the cohesive unit that Don was trying to develop; they started helping one another instead of trying to impress each other. We've never taught a class composed entirely of youngsters, and it would undoubtedly present some unique problems for the instructor, but it just would have to be fun. Every class should have a kid or two present just to help break down the adults' reserve and to keep them on their toes.

If working directly with people is something that you really enjoy, you might consider seeing your local fly shop or sporting goods store and try to interest them in allowing you to teach a class. It is challenging, interesting, and can really be fun for the teacher. Make sure, however, that you have fully planned what you are going to cover and how you are going to do it so that the student is led (always) from the very simple to the more difficult steps while his interest is maintained. One other point and it is an important one: The truly professional instructor is always open-minded to other ways of accomplishing a given step or technique because he is aware that there are many ways of achieving a particular result. Above all, the professional has no need to be critical of another's approach to fly-tying; the instructor who succumbs to the temptation to criticise and condemn other tyers is quickly perceived by his students to be unsure of himself.

There are several benefits that are accrued by the instructor: a few bucks, some prestige, a feeling of accomplishment, and the development of some real friendships. Probably the biggest benefit though is what you will learn about fly-tying. It has often been said that if you really want to learn something, then teach it. You will discover how you *really* tie when you have to explain it to someone else, you will find shortcuts that you never thought of, simply because you are seeing the tying process in greater detail than ever before. You will also find that your students, who aren't yet set into a particular method or approach to tying, will show you a few tricks that you have never thought of on your own.

Which, if either, of the two approaches into the ranks of the professional fly tyer that most appeals to you is dependent almost entirely on your personality. Neither the commercial tyer nor the instructor needs to be a "great" fly tyer in the beginning; either facet of professional tying will, in itself, develop the needed ability very quickly. The outgoing, gregarious individual is more likely to enjoy the teaching aspect, while the independent, hard-driving personality may be better suited to the role of a commercial tyer. It really isn't that cut-and-dried, however; we know tyers who fit into both categories and are equally proficient in either. One thing is sure though; time spent in either aspect of the professional fly tyer will serve to make you a better tyer.

Epilogue

He gripped my hand tightly as we crossed the shallow rapids; ten years old, small for his age, and wearing waders for the first time. Those waders had delayed this trip for most of the summer: the smallest that I could find had to be mail-ordered and, of course, were backordered. They still fit over his sneakers. His anxiety at being in fast water for the first time showed only in the firm hold on my hand and the white knuckles of his left hand grasping the seven-foot Fenwick that he was to *use* for the first time today.

When we reached the shallow rapids on the other shore, I set him up with a typical Colorado nymphing rig: a #14 buckskin nymph, one piece of wrap-on lead about twenty inches up, and a small strike indicator at the line/leader junction. After much thought, I had decided that this set-up was the most likely to meet with that all-important success on his first time out. Not that nymph fishing is easy, but because the chance of a trout taking the fly as it makes the swing at the end of the drift is pretty good, and the chance of the fish hooking itself is excellent.

After a few last reminders about waiting out the backcast, watching the strike indicator, and avoiding drag, I moved upstream. I picked a spot just far enough above him to be able to reach him quickly, and yet, for it to be obvious that he was accepted as being able to take care of himself.

I was releasing my second small fish when I heard the quiet splash of a rising trout just upstream. I watched the suspected stretch of water intently as I removed the fly and the strip of lead from the leader. As I was reaching for my dry-fly box, the rise came again; three feet out from the opposite bank, under overhanging bushes. Sporadic rises, overhanging brush, terrestrials? My fingers sought out a #16 Humpy. He was still doggedly casting when I glanced his way before making the first cast. The fly drifted untouched on the first cast, but on the second pass the trout sucked it in. As I played the fish in for the release, I took a quick look and saw that I was, indeed, being watched. One more trout quickly fell to the imitation and then, momentarily sated, I backed out of the stream.

I noticed now that there were several fish rising down near the boy. As I watched him make the next couple of casts, it was obvious that he had lost interest. He had noticed the rising fish across from where he stood and turned and looked at me with questioning eyes. I moved to his elbow and attached a Humpy to his tippet as I knelt beside him.

His first cast hit the water like a rope and I heard him sigh in disappointment. The second cast was better but just short of the needed drift line. The first cast had put down one of the feeders but he laid this cast on the water with some semblance of delicacy and the drift line looked good—but no take. He was tiring now; it showed in his lower backcast and poor timing; when the rise did come—he missed it! Instead of the expected look of disappointment though, he was elated. He had seen, actually seen, a fish rise to his fly. I suggested that we break for lunch and rest the pool.

We washed down bologna-and-cheese sandwiches with warm cola as we talked about "his" trout and trout fishing. He asked about the "Stop Two Forks Dam" bumper sticker on the car next to us. I explained that some people wanted to build a dam and flood this whole valley and that, yes, everyone who lived here would have to move and all of the cabins would be torn down. I agreed that is wasn't fair that maybe by the time he was old enough to drive up here by himself the river would be gone. We talked about the need to release the fish so that they would be here the next time that we came.

He crossed the rapids ahead of me this time, full of confidence and anxious to get back to his fish. I moved above him and watched as he made his first cast: he hadn't forgotten where to lay the fly and as it drifted down the feeding lane, the trout rose just behind it to take a natural.

A rise caught my attention and just as I made my second cast, I heard him whoop. The rod was bent and throbbing and his face showed as much bewilderment as excitement. Shouting instructions, I backed out of the pool and moved down to him. As he brought the trout in close, I asked if he wanted to keep it. "No, I want to catch him again someday," he said.

We released the fish and just stood looking at each other for a few seconds. "Let me shake your hand, Mace, you are now a fly fisherman. Remember this pool, son, remember what it looks like here, you'll never catch your first trout again; I can't remember mine and how I wish I could."

There was a long pause as he looked around. "Daddy, that was the most wonderful thing that has ever happened to me." Then he flew into my arms and wiped a mustard-stained cheek against mine—after all, he's only ten!

TAKE A KID FISHING!

APPENDIX

Selected Bibliography

Bates, Joseph D., Jr. *Streamer Fly-Tying and Fishing.* Harrisburg, PA: Stackpole Books, 1966.

Boyle, R. H., and Whitlock, D. *The Fly Tyer's Almanac.* New York: Crown, 1975.

————. *The Second Fly Tyer's Almanac.* Philadelphia: Lippincott, 1978.

Brooks, Charles E. *Nymph Fishing for Larger Trout.* New York: Crown, 1976.

————. *The Trout and the Stream.* New York: Crown, 1974.

Caucci, Al, and Natasi, Bob. *Hatches.* New York: Comparahatch, 1975.

Combs, Trey. *Steelhead Fly Fishing and Flies.* Portland: Frank Amato, 1976.

Dennis, Jack H., Jr. *Western Trout Fly Tying Manual.* Jackson Hole, WY: Snake River Books, 1974.

————. *Western Trout Fly Tying Manual, Vol. II.* Jackson Hole, WY: Snake River Books, 1980.

Flick, Art. *Art Flick's Master Fly Tying Guide.* New York: Crown, 1972.

Hellekson, Terry, *Popular Fly Patterns.* Salt Lake City: Peregrine Smith, 1977.

Jorgensen, Poul. *Dressing Flies for Fresh and Salt Water.* Rockville Centre, NY: Freshet Press, 1973.

————. *Modern Fly Dressings for the Practical Angler.* New York: Winchester Press, 1976.

————. *Salmon Flies.* Harrisburg PA: Stackpole Books, 1978.

Kaufmann, Randal. *American Nymph Fly Tying Manual.* Portland: Frank Amato, 1976.

LaFontaine, Gary. *Challenge of the Trout.* Missoula, MT: Mountain Press, 1976.

Leiser, Eric. *Fly Tying Materials.* New York: Crown, 1973.

Light, Tom, and Humphrey, Neal. *Steelhead Fly Tying Manual.* Portland: Frank Amato, 1980.

Migel, J. M. *Masters on the Dry Fly.* Philadelphia: Lippincott, 1977.

Migel, J. M. and Wright, L. *Masters on the Nymph.* Philadelphia: Lippincott, 1979.

Roberts, Donald V. *Flyfishing Still Waters*. Portland: Frank Amato, 1978.

Rosborough, E. H. *Tying and Fishing the Fuzzy Nymphs*. Harrisburg, PA: Stackpole Books, 1978.

Schwiebert, Ernest. *Matching the Hatch*. New York: Macmillan, 1974.

———. *Nymphs*. New York: Winchester Press, 1973.

———. *Trout*. New York: E. P. Dutton, 1978.

Surette, Dick. *Trout and Salmon Fly Index*. Harrisburg, PA: Stackpole Books, 1974.

Swisher, Doug, and Richards, Carl. *Selective Trout*. New York: Crown, 1971.

———. *Flyfishing Strategy*. New York: Crown, 1975.

———. *Tying the Swisher/Richards Flies*. Eugene, OR: P. J. Dillan, 1977.

In addition to the above books, all of which are important enough to be included in every fly tyer's library, we also strongly recommend the following magazines as the best means of keeping in touch with what is new in fly-tying.

Fly Tyer
Box 1231, Rt. 16
North Conway, NH   03860

Flyfishing the West
P.O. Box 02112
Portland, OR   97202

Fly Fisherman
Dorset, VT   05251

Sources of Materials and Supplies

HOOKS

O. Mustad & Son (USA) Inc.
P.O. Box 838
Auburn, NY   13021

Partridge of Redditch
Worcestershire, England B974JE

Wright & McGill Co.
4245 E. 46th St.
Denver, CO   80216

VMC Inc.
1482 W. County Rd. C
St. Paul, MN   55113

VISES

Angling Products Inc. (HMH)
116 Pleasant Ave.
Upper Saddle River, NJ   07458

The Bedford Sportsman, Inc. (Xuron)
25 Adams St.
Bedford Hills, NY   10507

D. H. Thompson, Inc.
11 N. Union St.
Elgin, IL   60120

Price's Angler's Corner
P.O. Box 356
LaPine, OR   97739

Regal Vise
P.O. Box 277
Harwichport, MA   02606

Mr. A. Renzetti
P.O. Box 322, Shadyside Rd.
RD #4
Coatesville, PA   19320

TOOLS

D. H. Thompson, Inc.
11 N. Union St.
Elgin, IL   60120

Hunter's
P.O. Box 55A
New Boston, NH   03070

J. D. Fly Tying Tool Co.
27544 Seco Cyn. Rd.
Saugus, CA   91350

Frank Matarelli
San Francisco, CA   94122

Mr. A. Renzetti
P.O. Box 322, Shadyside Rd.
RD #4
Coatesville, PA   19320

MATERIALS

Andra Co.
P.O. Box 137
Southport, CT   06490

Bob Jacklin's Fly Shop
P.O. Box 604
West Yellowstone, MT   59758

Buz's Fly and Tackle Shop
805 W. Tulare
Visalia, CA   93277

The Caddis Fly
450 Willamette St.
Eugene, OR   97401

Creative Angler
P.O. Box 545
Kirkland, WA   98033

Dan Bailey's Fly Shop
Livingston, MT   59047

Donegal
P.O. Box 979, Old Route 9W
Fort Montgomery, NY   10922

E. Hille
The Angler's Supply House
P.O. Box 996
Williamsport, PA   17701

F. A. Johnson, Inc. (Swannundaze®)
118 Rutherford Ave.
Lyndhurst, NJ   07071

Flyfisher's Paradise
P.O. Box 448
Lemont, PA   16851

Fly-Rite
7421 S. Beyer Rd.
Frankenmuth, MI   48734

The Hook & Hackle Company
P.O. Box 1003
Plattsburg, NY   12901

Hook & Hackle Industries Ltd.
P.O. Box 6
Lethbridge, Alberta
Canada   T1J3Y3

Hunter's
P.O. Box 55A
New Boston, NH   03070

Kaufmann's Streamborn Fly Shop
P.O. Box 23032
Portland, OR   97233

L&L Products, Inc. (Microweb)
12 Raemar Ct.
Bethpage, PA   11714

National Feather Craft Corp.
P.O. Box 186
Florissant, MO   63033

Phelps Flies Co. (Nymphorms)
P.O. Box 224
Katonah, NY   10536

Raymond C. Rumpf & Son
Ferndale, PA   18921

The Rivergate
RT. 9, Box 275
Cold Springs, NY   10516

Index